Solution-Focused Therapy

Brief Therapies Series

Series Editor: Stephen Palmer
Associate Editor: Gladeana McMahon

Focusing on brief and time-limited therapies, this series of books is aimed at students, beginning and experienced counsellors, therapists and other members of the helping professions who need to know more about working with the specific skills, theories and practices involved in this demanding but vital area of their work.

Books in the series:

*A Psychodynamic Approach to Brief
Counselling and Psychotherapy*
Gertrud Mander

Brief Cognitive Behaviour Therapy
Berni Curwen, Stephen Palmer and Peter Ruddell

Solution-Focused Groupwork
John Sharry

Brief NLP Therapy
Ian McDermott and Wendy Jago

Transactional Analysis Approaches to Brief Therapy
Keith Tudor

Handbook of Solution-Focused Therapy
edited by Bill O'Connell and Stephen Palmer

Brief Gestalt Therapy
Gaie Houston

Solution-Focused Therapy

Second Edition

Bill O'Connell

SAGE Publications
London ● Thousand Oaks ● New Delhi

First edition first published 1998
Reprinted 2000, 2001, 2003, 2004
This second edition first published 2005

SAGE Publications Ltd
1 Oliver's Yard
55 City Road
London EC1Y 1SP

SAGE Publications Inc.
2455 Teller Road
Thousand Oaks, California 91320

SAGE Publications India Pvt Ltd
B-42, Panchsheel Enclave
Post Box 4109
New Delhi 110 017

British Library Cataloguing in Publication data

A catalogue record for this book is available
from the British Library

ISBN 1-4129-0328-9
ISBN 1-4129-0329-7 (pbk)

Library of Congress Control Number available

Typeset by C&M Digitals (P) Ltd., Chennai, India
Printed on paper from sustainable resources
Printed in Great Britain by The Cromwell Press Ltd, Trowbridge, Wiltshire

To Moira, *cariad*

Contents

Foreword by Harvey Ratner   viii

Foreword by Alasdair J Macdonald   x

Preface to the Second Edition   xii

Acknowledgements for the First Edition   xvi

Acknowledgements for the Second Edition   xvii

1   Brief Therapy   1

2   Foundations of SFT   7

3   Overview of the Model   18

4   The First Session   37

5   Second Sessions and Beyond: Keeping
    the Focus on Solutions   64

6   The Solution-focused Practitioner   80

7   Solution-focused Supervision   89

8   Frequently Asked Questions About SFT   102

9   An Integrative Solution-focused Approach   114

10 Applying the Solution-focused Approach   131

Appendix: Solution-focused Resources   140

References   143

Index   150

Foreword by Harvey Ratner

Solution-focused therapy is a form of brief therapy that was first developed in the United States in the 1980s. It made its entrance into the UK at the end of the 1980s and, since then, thousands of therapists and counsellors in statutory and non-statutory services have been attracted to short training courses to learn how to use the deceptively simple methods of the approach. A similar movement is taking place across Europe, with therapists in Sweden, Germany, France, Belgium and other countries defining their principal approach as solution-focused brief therapy.

There are of course many different reasons for this therapy having become so popular at this time. Among its attractions, to judge by evaluation forms from training courses, is not only the practical nature of the techniques but also its client-centredness, specifically its focus on competency and strength in clients rather than their assumed deficits and pathology. There seems to be a growing move towards working in partnership with clients, to help them establish what they want to be different in their lives and seek out the strengths they have for accomplishing those changes. This therefore fits well with research that shows clients, when asked for their opinion on what helps them in therapy, refer most often to a relationship of trust in which they feel heard – and what better way to develop that than to focus the therapy on what the *client* wants?

It is therefore a pleasure to welcome a valuable addition to the growing collection of writings worldwide that reflect the use of solution-focused therapy. It is doubly pleasing to welcome a book as clear and well written as Bill O'Connell's. Throughout he offers the reader short, readable examples of different facets of the approach that make the material as accessible as possible. In particular, he is able to present complicated ideas about the background to the approach in a straightforward and succinct manner.

O'Connell tells us that he comes from an eclectic background, and this is demonstrated in his arguments for an integrated approach. Many readers will find Chapter 9, An Integrative Solution-focused Approach, to be of great value in the way it makes connections between solution-focused brief therapy and other counselling approaches. It teems with useful tips from different approaches and will have something for most people. He also has interesting things to say about adapting the ideas to other settings, such as groups and organizations (see Chapter 10, Applying the Solution-focused Approach) and his chapter on frequently asked questions (Chapter 8) offers some clear and convincing replies to thorny issues.

With his years of practising and teaching counselling skills, it is perhaps inevitable that O'Connell is particularly astute in describing the ingredients of the relationship between therapist and client that are most conducive to a brief approach. Those working as counsellors will find this book, and Chapter 6 in particular, of especial relevance to their work.

The reason, I would guess, that you are holding this book is that you are interested in brief approaches to therapy that have the aim of empowering clients to take control of their own problem-solving abilities. You will find suggestions and strings-to-your-bow aplenty here!

Harvey Ratner
Brief Therapy Practice, London

Foreword by Alasdair J Macdonald

When the first edition of this book was published in 1998 few of the publications about solution-focused brief therapy had originated in the United Kingdom. At that time the majority of the books had been written in the United States by the founders of the approach, Steve de Shazer and Insoo Kim Berg, or by their trainees and colleagues. Bill O'Connell's academic credentials and his easy writing style contributed to the success of *Solution-Focused Therapy*. The book found a readership among existing solution-focused practitioners and appealed to many therapists who were seeking an introduction to the exciting possibilities offered by the solution-focused approach. Since then the book has been recommended as a text for university and college courses and by the influential Brief Therapy Practice (now BRIEF) in London. The call for a second edition testifies both to the rapid expansion of solution-focused practice in the United Kingdom and to the value of the book itself.

Solution-focused therapy itself is a rising star in the therapy firmament around the world. Its ideas and methods have spread to many countries throughout the Western world and are now increasing their influence in India and the Far East. Meetings of the European Brief Therapy Association usually have representatives from 20 or 30 countries. In the United Kingdom solution-focused therapy ideas are prominent in education and social work as well as within the NHS and the private sector. The approach has proved effective in some areas of practice which have traditionally been seen as difficult or impossible for psychological work such as domestic violence, child protection and drug use. This rapid expansion is demonstrated by the growth in calls for solution-focused supervision, leading to the inclusion in this second edition of new material on this issue in Chapter 7. Solution-focused concepts are being widely used and taught in organisational work by management consultants from many backgrounds. The Solution-focused Reflecting Team's technique for supervision and organisational work forms additional new matter in the present edition (Chapter 7).

As Bill points out in the Preface, solution-focused brief therapy is still developing and changing. It has roots in family therapy but is also indebted to other therapies including psychodynamic, behavioural and person-centred approaches. It is one measure of the success of the method that many other established therapies are beginning to talk of collaboration, empowerment, self-esteem and hope. Previously these concepts were rarely mentioned in the literature concerning the management of emotional distress and mental disorder. Preliminary research suggests that therapists enjoy their work more once they become solution-oriented, which may reduce 'burn-out' and is therefore a good omen for the future development of the therapy profession. Finland has accepted solution-focused therapy as a formal school of therapy and the United Kingdom Association for Solution Focused Practice, like similar organisations in other countries, is examining the possibility of achieving formal accreditation for solution-focused therapy. This will put it on an equal footing with other well-established schools of therapy around the world.

There are many clients and many therapists around the world who have gained something from solution-focused approaches. This second edition of *Solution-focused Therapy* will allow and encourage many more successes and developments. So if you have picked this book up in a bookshop, buy it! It might change your professional life, as it has done for many others.

Dr Alasdair J Macdonald
Consultant Psychiatrist
President, European Brief Therapy Association

Preface to the Second Edition

The first edition of *Solution-Focused Therapy* was published in 1998. Since then, the popularity of the approach has grown and it now enjoys support from a wide range of practitioners. It has been creatively adapted and applied in many different contexts – from business organisations to parent support groups. Many of those who use the approach do not have a background in therapy and may even be unaware of its origins in family therapy. This edition, although primarily aimed at counsellors and therapists, is designed also for other disciplines and professions.

There has been a geographical expansion, too, with many exponents of the approach in Scandinavia, Holland and Germany, as well as in the United Kingdom and the United States of America. Practitioners have also organised themselves more collectively with, for example, the launch of the United Kingdom Association of Solution Focused Practice in 2003, a similar organisation in the United States and the continuing popular success of the European Brief Therapy Association. These organisations are doing a great deal to promote good practice and develop creative applications of the approach.

The solution-focused perspective is now found on the curricula of many professional training courses, such as psychology and social work. It has been recognised in the UK's National Health Service as an effective and valid therapeutic intervention. It has achieved academic respectability, with the University of Birmingham in the UK offering an MA in Solution-Focused Therapy since 1999. The course has attracted an interdisciplinary student group from the UK and mainland Europe. There are increasing numbers of trainers and consultants who teach solution-focused ideas and interventions to staff in private, voluntary and public-sector organisations. Also, many coaches and mentors are using the approach with their clients.

This edition reflects the latest developments in the field – one of which is the renewed emphasis on client empowerment. The therapist/interviewer takes a back seat, although an important one. Another shift is towards greater simplicity or minimalism with maximum flexibility of application. In this edition, there are fewer 'shoulds, oughts and musts' about implementing the therapeutic process, which reflects a greater trust in the clients' ability to find and implement their solutions. I have strengthened the chapter on supervision by introducing a model for one-to-one supervision, as well as an extended section on the running of solution-focused reflecting teams. There are practice points at the end of each chapter and a more comprehensive list of resources in the Appendix.

The practice of the solution-focused approach is never static. Each time I attend a conference or seminar I am struck with how inventive and original its practitioners are. As a relatively new kid on the block, solution-focused therapy (SFT) is unencumbered by the weight of great tradition. In fact, there is a great sense of excitement that everything is a 'work in progress'. There is a strong collective identity, too, that encourages each person to make a contribution to the development of the work. One cannot fail to be struck by the enthusiasm, commitment and passion in any gathering of solution-focused students or trainees. Finding the solution-focused approach has been a turning point in the lives of many people. It has set them off on personal and professional journies from which there has been no going back.

There are few gurus and even fewer tablets of stone in the solution-focused field. Although the first generation of original thinkers – for example, de Shazer, Kim Berg, O'Hanlon – are received with great respect, they do not occupy god-like positions. There is a strong rebellious streak among the body of those who make up solution-focused practitioners. This showed itself when they critically challenged more established therapies in order to embrace a more radical, egalitarian model. This energy continues to fuel the solution-focused movement and prevents it from ossifying.

While the benefits to clients are clear from the research findings, it is also the case that those who practice the approach feel that there are benefits for them as well. Sundmann (1997) reported that social workers using the approach in Finland made more positive statements about their clients and worked more collaboratively with them than those who did not. In my experience, the more I use the model, the more I warm to my clients. It helps me to appreciate what they are doing to overcome their difficulties. I know from colleagues how much the positive, optimistic and hopeful values in the approach have served as antidotes to the negativity, fatalistic cynicism and burnout that can result from listening to other people's problems for many hours.

People read books differently. Those whose preferred learning style is practical may choose to start with the chapters that describe the use of the approach – namely Chapters 3, 4, 5 and 6. Those who find it helpful to have the historical context and theoretical foundations may prefer to start at the beginning. Solution-focused supervision is the central theme of Chapter 7, while in Chapter 8 I have attempted to answer a series of questions about the model. Chapter 9 examines how SFT could be integrated with other models, and finally, in Chapter 10, I describe the ways in which it is used in a variety of settings.

Throughout, I have alternated the use of female and male pronouns – hopefully in a way that avoids gender stereotyping. I have also used the terms 'counselling' and 'therapy' and 'counsellor' and 'therapist' interchangeably, in accordance with the practice of the British Association for Counselling and Psychotherapy. In some chapters I use the terms 'counsellor' and 'therapist' exclusively, but in others I have used the inclusive term 'practitioner' to cover anyone working in a helping capacity, whether they would regard themselves as therapists or counsellors or not.

The Latin root of the word solution is *solvere*, the verb to release. In that sense, I like to think of SFT as a form of 'liberation', an experience that enables people to release themselves from the tyranny of their pasts. I also like to think that it releases practitioners to treat their clients as equals and affirm and celebrate all that is best about people. On the other hand, there are overtones to the title *Solution-Focused Therapy* that give the impression there is a solution for every problem, which leads its critics to dismiss it as a 'quick fix' therapy. My preference would be a title such as 'Change-Focused Therapy' or 'Future-Orientated Therapy'.

I also understand the suspicion that many people in the field have that brief interventions conveniently provide a rationale for funders to cut budgets. However, the research base for brief therapy is strong and the reality on the ground is that a lot of the counselling/therapy offered in the UK is, in practice, brief.

It is not only the funders who are promoting brief interventions but also the clients themselves. They are saying that they benefit from time-limited help and prefer it to a long-term commitment. Provided that brief therapy is not the only treatment option sanctioned, I take the view that practitioners who want to make the best possible use of resources and extend their services to clients currently denied them, will welcome the advent of brief therapy. I believe that we need to offer our clients a service that is congruent with their circumstances and preferences, and we need to be accountable to them and to the wider community for the effectiveness of what we do.

My own background is in youth work, social work and counselling as well as training and lecturing. My experience comes mainly from working with individual clients and couples. I have used the model with a wide range of clients in various settings – a student counselling service, voluntary agency offering family and couples counselling, private practice and employee assistance programmes.

Some solution-focused therapists use the model in a purist, way, while others are open to integrating it with other models. Coming from an eclectic background, I belong to the latter school and it is my hope that this book will appeal to a broad spectrum of therapists who are open to incorporating new ideas into their practice. This book does not imply criticism of models used by other practitioners, although I question the need for long-term therapy for all but a minority of clients. The solution-focused principle – if it works keep doing it – is a pragmatic signal to continue with whichever approach we are using if it is working for our clients.

However, where it is not working, we need to be brave enough to do something else. No therapy always works and the more tools we have in the toolbox the better, provided we know and understand why we are using them. The current climate in therapy today encourages us to adopt an eclectic, developmental attitude to our own work. The movement towards consensus and respect for diversity is replacing the sterile polemics of therapy politics and it is in this spirit that the book is written. I have tried to acknowledge the limitations of the approach as well as its potential. When any approach places a heavy emphasis on a certain type of intervention – which, in the case of SFT, means the use of questions – it inevitably neglects interventions used in other types of therapy. Followers of other therapies will therefore be sensitive to what is not done in SFT as well be surprised at times by what is done. No therapy claims to do everything, however, and it is misleading to judge one therapy on the basis of what happens in others. Some critics dismiss SFT as being somewhat lightweight in terms of ideology, yet the philosophical underpinning is conceptually difficult to grasp and the simplicity of practice is rarely easy! It requires considerable relationship skills, as well as the ability to focus on what is positive and non-problematic for the client. The novice practitioner, therefore, unencumbered by conflicting ideologies, may find it easier to practise in a solution-focused way than someone coming to it with a lot of intellectual baggage. In some cases, too, people with non-counselling backgrounds who work in settings that require counselling skills take enthusiastically to the solution-focused approach as it strikes them as practical and accessible. They are relieved that they do not have to be problem solvers. However, in my opinion, for those planning to work as counsellors or therapists, it can be helpful to have undergone a generalist counselling training first.

I hope that this book helps you to enjoy what you do, gives you lots of ideas for working with clients and helps you to listen more for your clients' solutions.

Acknowledgements for the First Edition

I would like to express my sincere thanks to those people who made this book possible. In the first place, my warmest thanks go to my wife Moira, my grown-up daughters Donnamarie, Joanne and Katrina for the love and support they have always given me. I also owe a great debt of gratitude to my colleague Janet Bellamy at Westhill College for all her help, and also to Clare Austin and Joyce Colwell. I am especially grateful to the many students and clients who have taught me so much over the years. May I thank John Wheeler for his constructive and informed comments throughout the writing of the book and for his and his colleagues' help in collecting together the useful website addresses for the Appendix; Harvey Ratner and his colleagues at the Brief Therapy Practice for their encouragement; and Gladeana McMahon and Stephen Palmer for their support.

Acknowledgements for the Second Edition

I would like to express my sincere thanks to all those who have contributed to the production of this second edition. I wish to thank my colleagues at Sage for all their help – to Alison Poyner for her faith in the book, to Louise Wise for her warm support and to Rachel Burrows and her colleagues for their work on improving the manuscript. Thanks also to Stephen Palmer who has championed my writing of Solution-Focused books.

I am grateful to Alasdair Macdonald for adding an updated foreword to this edition. Alasdair has been an immense figure in the development of Solution-Focused work in the UK and I and many others are in his debt. May I also thank my associates in Focus on Solutions – Steve Conlon, Peter Creagh and Vicky Bliss for their generous sharing of ideas. Over the past few years it has been my privilege to introduce many hundreds of people to Solution-Focused ideas and practice. Their creative and enthusiastic engagement with the approach has taught me a great deal.

As ever my thanks go to my family. To my grown up children – Donnamarie, Joanne and Katrina whose varied interests mean they have become their father's teachers. Finally, may I thank my wife Moira who continues to offer her total support in all aspects of my life. Her contribution to this edition has been crucial. Her clarity of thought, her wisdom and compassion have made this a much better book than it would otherwise have been.

1
Brief Therapy

The unique feature of solution-focused therapy (SFT) is that it focuses on solutions, not problems. It aims to help clients achieve their preferred outcomes by evoking and co-constructing solutions to their problems (O'Connell, 2001). It emerged in the 1980s as a form of brief therapy, with its origins in the work of Steve de Shazer and his team at the Brief Family Therapy Center in Milwaukee, USA. To understand its context, it is helpful to be aware of the brief therapy tradition.

The fact that many brief therapy models come from within the main schools of therapy (psychodynamic and cognitive behaviour in particular) can give the impression that brief therapy is a derivative of long-term therapy. However, this is not the case. Bloom (1992) lists a large number of case studies over the past 80 years in which patients report significant changes in their lives as a result of brief therapy. As far back as 1925, eminent therapists, such as Ferenczi and Rank, argued against the assumption that analysis had to be lengthy. They advocated that the therapist adopt an active empathic stance in making interpretations, promoting transference and keeping the emotional temperature high. Rank emphasised the importance of the client's motivation to engage in a process of change, the need to set an end to treatment and the necessity to pay more attention to the current experiences of the client rather than a reliving of the past. However, the psychoanalytic community remained defensive and hostile to the idea that therapy which was not lengthy and 'deep' could be of any lasting value. Alexander and French (1946) provoked considerable hostility when they wrote about the 'almost superstitious belief among psychoanalysts that quick therapeutic results cannot be genuine'. They had recommended using weekly rather than daily sessions to enable clients to put into practice what they had learned in therapy.

Malan's influential studies (1963, 1976) demonstrated the efficacy of short-term dynamic therapy. He highlighted the need for careful assessments and the need to retain a therapeutic focus for the work. From the 1960s to the 1980s the works of Malan, Mann (1973) Sifneos (1979) and Davanloo (1980) were the driving forces behind the case for brief dynamic casework. Since then, the increasing body of research demonstrating that brief therapy is equally as effective as long term (summarised in Koss and Butcher, 1986), and that brief therapy is the expectation and preference for more than 70 per cent of clients (Garfield and Bergin, 1994;

Pekarik, 1991), has been a powerful market force. Frances, Clarkin and Perry (1984) found that a wide range of practitioners – marital therapists, sex therapists, family therapists, crisis therapists and cognitive-behavioural therapists – all claimed to work within a short period of time and that their actual practice bore this out. One study of a counselling centre in the UK (Brech and Agulnik, 1996) found that approximately 40 per cent of clients had between one and four sessions, a further 40 per cent between five and 20, and 20 per cent had therapy contracts extending beyond 6 months. The study found that by introducing a four-session model for clients on the waiting list, the number waiting was reduced and this reduced the waiting time for all clients, even those who had not accepted the offer of four sessions and who chose to wait for more open-ended therapy. The majority of studies over recent decades show that the median length of treatment of whatever orientation ranges from four to eight sessions, with a clustering around six (Garfield and Bergin, 1994; Koss and Butcher, 1986). Koss and Butcher (1986) conclude that 'almost all psychotherapy is brief.'

There are differences in definition as to what constitutes brief therapy. Eckert (1993) defined brief therapy as being 'any psychological intervention intended to produce change as quickly as possible whether or not a specific time limit is set in advance.' Malan (1976), from a psychodynamic tradition, used the term to mean between four and 50 sessions; Mann (1973), from the same tradition, set a fixed number of 12; while Ryle's (1991) cognitive-analytic model used 16. Talmon (1990) and Manthei (1996) argued the case for single-session therapy. While some models set fixed limits, others are brief within flexible parameters (Steenbarger, 1994). Budman and Gurman (1988) prefer the term 'time-sensitive therapy', which they feel highlights the need for the therapist to make maximum impact within a rationed amount of time. Although there are major differences between brief therapists, there is a degree of consensus that brief therapy means fewer than 20 sessions.

There is considerable agreement in the literature about the main characteristics of planned brief therapy. These features are also prominent in solution-focused brief therapy. Barret-Kruse (1994) summarises them as follows:

- the view that yourself and others are essentially able
- the acceptance of the client's definition of the problem
- the formation of the therapeutic alliance
- crediting the client with the success
- the therapist learning from the client
- the avoidance of a power struggle with the client
- the objectification, rather than the personalisation, of the client's behaviour.

She asserts that in brief therapy the therapist needs to join with the client in creating an expectancy of change. In her view, this requires a degree of directiveness from the therapist in order to form a working relationship as quickly as possible. It is equally important to identify the problem and the goal(s) clearly and develop appropriate action plans that are carefully evaluated. In brief therapy, the client defines the problem. Wells and Gianetti (1993) argue that a collaborative and effective relationship can be established more quickly if clients receive as much information about the problem and the therapy as possible.

Koss and Butcher (1986) summarise the research by describing the main features of brief therapy as being:

- a focus on the here and now
- clear, specific and attainable goals achievable in the time available
- the establishment of a good working relationship as soon as possible
- the projection of the therapist as competent, hopeful and confident
- the therapist is being active and openly influential.

In contrast, Hoyt (1995) identifies a number of beliefs that underpin long-term therapy:

- damaging early experiences must be slowly and fully uncovered
- the therapeutic alliance must form gradually
- the client must be allowed to regress
- transference takes a long time to develop and must not be interpreted too early
- consolidation of gains requires a lengthy period of working through.

Effectiveness

The research evidence for the effectiveness of brief therapy is impressive. Kogan (1957) followed up clients three and 12 months after they had received a single session of therapy. Approximately two-thirds felt that they had been helped. He concluded that, in cases with unplanned endings, therapists consistently underestimated the help clients had received. Malan, Heath, Bacal and Balfour (1975), in a study of 45 clients, two to eight years after they had received a single session of therapy, found that a quarter had improved symptomatically and another quarter had also improved in dynamic terms. Smith (1980) found that the major impact of therapy occurred in the first six to eight sessions, followed by a continuing but decreasing positive impact for approximately the next ten sessions. Howard, Kopta, Krause and Orlinsky (1986), in a meta-study, found that 15 per cent of clients improved before the first session, 50 per cent by the eighth, 75 per cent by the twenty-sixth and 83 per cent by the fifty-second. Stern (1993) suggests that those who stay longer are those who do not feel that they have made enough progress. Brech and Agulnik (1996) found that, of clients who received four planned sessions of therapy in a setting that used psychodynamic methods, 25 per cent found it useful and sufficient and, for a further 50 per cent, it was a useful beginning that helped them to plan the possibility of further long-term work. Bloom (1992) concluded that short-term psychotherapies were equally effective as time-unlimited psychotherapy.

Howard and his colleagues' meta-study (1986) suggests that, although frequency of sessions was not related to improvement, the structuring of therapy is important because clients can use regular sessions as organising factors in their lives. It can be helpful to have special times assigned for themselves and, in addition, there must be a degree of intensity in sessions for change to take place.

It is not clear whether therapy is brief because it works or it works because it is brief. Perry (1987) suggests that the effectiveness of brief therapies may be due to the techniques used, rather than to the short duration of the therapy itself.

In 1990 Talmon published his influential study on single-session therapy. He researched over 10,000 outpatients of a psychiatric hospital who had received psychotherapy. He discovered that the most frequent length of therapy was one session and that 30 per cent of all patients chose to come for only one session in a period of a year, irrespective of the theoretical orientation of the therapist. Moreover, in a follow-up study of 200 of his own clients, 78 per cent said that they had received what they had wanted from a single session. In another study of planned single-session therapy he found that 88 per cent of clients reported that they had improved since the first session and 79 per cent thought that the single session had been enough. His study challenged the view that clients who leave therapy early are failed dropouts. He claimed that his research indicated brief therapy was the preferred choice of many clients and more therapy need not necessarily mean more effective therapy. As Hoyt (1995: 144) puts it, 'More is not necessarily better. Better is better.'

Research into solution-focused therapy

The most comprehensive, up-to-date review of SFT outcome research was conducted by Gingerich and Eisengart (2000 – a summary of which can be found on Gingerich's website at www.gingerich.net/SFBT/research/Default.htm). Of the 18 controlled outcome studies, he classified seven as being strongly controlled, five as moderately controlled and six as weakly controlled. Of the 18 studies, 17 reported client improvement, 10 of which were statistically significant. Further, seven of the 11 studies that compared solution-focused behaviour therapy with other standard treatments reported at least equivalent results. The range of strongly controlled studies covered depression in college students, groups in schools, parenting skills, rehabilitation of orthopeadic patients, recidivism in a prison population, antisocial behaviour of adolescent offenders and hopefulness among depressed clients.

Kiser (1988) and De Jong and Hopwood's (1996) studies of the Brief Family Therapy Centre in Milwaukee (de Shazer's team) found that:

- more than three-quarters of clients fully met their treatment goals or made progress towards them
- the average number of sessions was 3.0
- the counselling was equally effective with a diversity of clients and did not vary according to the client–counsellor gender or racial mix
- the same therapeutic procedures were effective across a wide range of client-identified problems.

In the UK, Macdonald (1994) researched the patients of a psychiatric out-patient department in which all the counsellors had received solution-focused training. In a follow-up study a year after treatment, a positive outcome was self-reported in 70 per cent of patients (71 per cent by their GPs), while 10 per cent of patients reported a negative outcome. There was a significant correlation between positive outcome and the length of treatment. The mean number of sessions for the improved group was 5.47 and, for the unimproved, 3.71. Long-standing problems did slightly less well. Those in the group who deteriorated were younger and all were female. Social class was not a factor, perhaps suggesting that brief therapy is accessible to a wide range of people and may be effective for those groups thought to be apprehensive of traditional forms of therapy.

There is anecdotal evidence that the model brings about change in clients, but limited published research acceptable to the academic community. The development of a Europe-wide SFT research group will hopefully remedy this deficiency.

Consumer preference

Intermittent therapy – which is analogous to visiting a doctor from time to time as and when needed – is more in tune with how people currently live their live than traditional forms of therapy. Cummings and Sayama (1995) argue for intermittent therapy throughout the lifecycle. In their opinion, brief, focused therapy, which can be accessed at points of crisis during a person's life, is more effective than other models. There is evidence, as we have seen, that brief therapy is the therapy of choice for consumers. According to Pekarik and Wierzbicki's research (1986), 65 per cent of therapists preferred to deliver long-term therapy (more than 15 sessions), whereas only 20 per cent of their clients expected it. This may suggest that clients do not see themselves as being entitled to lengthy therapy, although that may be their preference; or it might point to clients not wanting to be *in* therapy, but, rather, choosing to go *through* it as quickly as possible. There is some evidence that clients opt for brief therapy even when they are entitled to lengthier periods of therapy at no cost to themselves (Hoyt, 1995). Such findings have clear implications for the just distribution of scarce therapy resources.

Clients' and therapists' understandings of the therapeutic process are very different. Llewelyn (1988) found that clients were motivated to find a solution to their problems and to feel better, whereas therapists prioritised the search for explanations for the problem and its transformation by means of insight. There is also evidence that clients' expectations about outcomes differ from those of many therapists. Warner (1996) suggested that counsellors find it difficult to believe that clients have benefited from brief interventions. According to Beutler and Crago (1987), the majority of clients are hoping for symptom relief whereas therapists plan to achieve character change in their clients.

In short, we need to recognise that brief therapy does not mean less of the same, as if it were a bargain basement offering, but that it has its own unique structure and process requiring different values and skills from the therapist (Barkham, 1993).

Practice points

- Use every session with a client, including the first, as if it were the last.
- Project confidence and hope that much can be achieved in limited time.
- Stay close to the client's agenda.
- Trust the competence of your client and keep out of his or her way.
- Ask yourself what difference it would make to your practice if you really believed that, 'more is not better, better is better.'
- Consider ways of evaluating the effectiveness of your work.

2

Foundations of SFT

When the invention of the steam engine was first announced in the last century, a distinguished scientist and wit is reported to have remarked: 'It works in practice, but does it work in theory?'

(quoted in O'Hanlon and Wilk, 1987)

In this chapter I shall explore the clinical and philosophical roots of the solution-focused approach. As its origins lie in the field of family therapy, this chapter will refer specifically to therapy, but, as we have already indicated, its application reaches beyond the narrow arena of therapy to any field of work that involves interpersonal interactions.

The team at the Brief Family Therapy Center (BFTC) in Milwaukee – the founders of the solution-focused therapy (SFT) – claim that the model evolved from clinical practice (de Shazer, Berg, Lipchik, Nunnally, Molnar, Gingerich and Weiner-Davis, 1986). They discovered that their clients made progress by talking about their preferred futures without analysing their 'problem-laden' histories. Clients felt empowered as they described what they wanted to happen in their lives (solutions). These solutions involved more than just the absence of the problem. The clinical team learnt that 'solutions' did not have to fit 'problems' – they had to fit the clients.

They found that by means of a questioning process, they could elicit clear ideas for change from clients. These questions – described by de Shazer (1985) as 'skeleton keys', – invited clients to:

- become more aware of exceptions – times when they succeeded in overcoming their problems
- utilise their personal and social resources
- imagine their preferred future – the miracle question
- take small steps forward.

These questions were strongly orientated towards the future, not the past, on the basis that 'the future does not exist and cannot be predicted. It must be imagined and invented' (Gelatt, 1989).

The discovery that future-orientated interventions empowered clients revolutionised the team's practice. In numerous articles and books, de Shazer described how members of the team tested interventions designed to facilitate solution talk (de Shazer, 1984; de Shazer, 1985; de Shazer and Molnar, 1984; de Shazer et al., 1986). By staying close to their clients' agendas, they began to develop strong collaborative relationships with their clients. They encouraged clients to focus on what was changeable and attainable instead of allowing the size and complexity of the problem to deskill and disempower them. The team was sceptical of the problem labels clients or their referrers brought with them, preferring instead to concentrate more on non-problematical behaviour and client competence, in the belief that people tend to behave well when treated well and act competently when they are treated as competent.

The BFTC team members emphasised the importance of learning from the client how to do the work. As they reflected on their experiences with clients, they began to develop a philosophical and epistemological rationale. In particular, de Shazer began to publish their research. In this chapter I will attempt to describe the philosophy behind the approach.

Schwartz (1955) identified three stages through which new theories pass.

1   In the first stage – the Essentialist – there are many competing schools, each claiming superiority. Their followers tend to be evangelical, narrow and intolerant zealots. This stage lasts until the flaws and limitations of the theory appear and/or it becomes integrated into the body of established practices.
2   In the second stage – the Transitional – the followers themselves begin to recognise limitations to their model. This can result in civil war between the progressives who accept these new insights and the orthodox who 'defend the faith' and see themselves as the true believers. They may retreat into the Essentialist stage. A dialectical tension between the two extremes may produce a centre party.
3   The third stage – the Ecological – is a process of integrating with other ideas, accompanied by an understanding of the constantly evolving nature of the field. In this stage, a more eclectic position may emerge.

This sequence of events often applies to new models of therapy as they seek to find their places in a competitive marketplace. Converts to a new approach may, like converts to any cause, deter rather than win new devotees by being too strident in their testimony and evangelism. I hope in later chapters to avoid this by showing how solution-focused ideas and interventions can be integrated into the repertoire of therapists, whatever their orientation, and also to acknowledge its limitations. It is not only therapists who find the solution-focused approach helpful but also many others who work to support people – coaches, mentors, teachers, nurses, substance misuse workers, youth workers and many others. The approach can be adapted to fit many different contexts and client groups.

Epistemology

In understanding theories of therapy it is essential to address the philosophical and epistemological positions that underlie them. Lynch (1996) identifies three perspectives on knowledge and reality available to the counsellor and researcher. The first perspective, a modern position, argues that there is an objective reality, of which we can have objective knowledge by virtue of our use of reason. This is the stance taken by the scientific/ medical model, with its emphasis on testing hypotheses by rational analysis of cause and effect.

The second, a social constructionist postmodern perspective, claims that there is no objective meaning to reality and all meaning is a human creation influenced by social and cultural factors. As language is a public phenomenon, our knowledge of reality is shaped by the linguistic context in which it is used. What was previously considered a definitive 'truth' was actually the dominant discourse of the powerful. Historically in the Western world, this meant a white, male, heterosexual viewpoint. Other views of the world, such as black, female, or gay, were regarded as deviations from the norm. The postmodern position takes a critical, anti-authoritarian stance towards Establishment dogmas. It is pragmatic and pluralistic in its approach.

The third perspective, which emphasises context, takes the view that there *is* an objective order and meaning in reality, but we are unable to know it because we are always constrained by our social context.

Practitioners vary in terms of how aware or committed they are to these epistemological stances. Their lack of awareness does not alter the fact that their practice inevitably makes many epistemological assumptions. While the current prevalence of pragmatic attitudes within psychotherapy is more creative than the narrow, defensive and polemical mentality that has characterised much of the history of psychotherapy, failure to pay rigorous attention to theoretical assumptions can lead to largely technical practice divorced from the ideological root from which it sprang. Just as a particular artifact found in an archaeological dig derives its meaning from its relationship to other items found on the site, understanding particular therapeutic interventions only comes from an attention to context – the bigger picture.

SFT belongs to the constructionist school of therapies, included among which are Kelly's personal construct theory (1955), neuro-linguistic programming (Bandler and Grinder, 1979), the brief problem-solving model developed at the Mental Research Institute (MRI) in Palo Alto in California by Watzlawick, Weakland and Fisch (1974) and the narrative approach described by White and Epston (1990). The MRI and the SFT model owed much to the seminal thinking of Gregory Bateson (1972) and Milton Erickson (1980).

Constructionism

In ancient Greece, the word *theoria* referred to a privileged group of male citizens who attended ritual cultic events, the athletic games and major public ceremonies. Their report back to the rest of the populace was considered to be 'the truth' about these occasions.

We use the term 'theory' to mean a speculative explanation for particular realities – it is a framework for making sense of information. The social constructionist epistemology that underpins SFT critiques the power claimed by the *theoria* to be the one, true interpreter of reality. Constructionism argues that meaning is created in the process of social interaction and negotiation. We have no direct access to objective truth independent of our linguistically constructed versions of reality. Theories are not objective versions of an external reality, but socially constructed views that emerge within a cultural, political and social context. According to Walter and Peller (1996: 14):

> The implications of seeing meaning-making as a social event of at least two selves while at the same time realizing that language is not tied to an objective reality, are that in a conversation there are at least two stories, at least two constructions, and a mutual, coordinated construction process.

No one person or school of thought possesses more of 'the truth' than another, so, the therapist, while having the expertise to guide the process, does not have access to truths that the client cannot access. As Allen (1993: 31) writes:

> The social constructionist values not knowing – knowledge is created out of conversations. There can be no drawing of irrevocable conclusions which are substantiated by selectively gathering and attending to data which support the theory.

The knower actively participates in constructing what is observed. According to Segal (1986), constructionism challenges our belief that reality exists independently of us, the observers. It undermines our wish for reality to be discoverable, predictable and certain. Constructionism claims that this inseparability of the known from the knower destroys the myth of absolute truth and the rigid dogmas that accompany it. Von Foerster's puzzle demonstrates the point by presenting us with a sentence and inviting us to fill in the missing word:

This sentence has ... letters.

The answer must include itself in the number of letters and there could be different answers depending on which number is chosen. You could not choose just any number, as there are already 22 letters before you insert your chosen number. In other words, there are different 'correct' answers to the problem (Segal, 1986).

Constructionism claims to present us with a much richer, more diverse way of looking at our world – one in which we have greater choices. In therapeutic interactions, the client and the therapist explore an extensive repertoire of meanings in order to negotiate a provisional understanding. This does not mean that any explanation for a 'problem' will suffice, but it underlines the subjectivity and cultural relativity of the language we use to describe our realities. Therapy becomes a dialogue in which both partners construct the problem and the solution. It is a game of linguistic chess. The 'problem' (which now is placed in postmodern quotation marks) does not carry an objective, fixed meaning that clients bring with them. Instead, they tell and retell their story using language that reshapes the social reality by which they live. In Watzlawick's phrase (1984), 'reality is invented, not discovered'. Language does not reflect reality, it creates it.

Historically, a structuralist representational view of language has dominated therapy. In this view, the task of the therapist is to get 'behind' or 'beneath' the client's language in order to discover its meaning. The interventions the therapist uses depend on her philosophical and epistemological stance with regard to knowledge, pathology and the nature of the human person. In the structural approach, language represents 'real' things out there, which have an objectivity independent of our knowledge of them – for example, concepts such as personality, behaviour, self-esteem. From this perspective, the skilled therapist's task is to help the client find this lost 'truth', which will confer meaning on the client's experience. The enlightenment arising from this discovery will hopefully guide and motivate the client to living more resourcefully. The quest for the 'truth' of the client's life will take different paths according to whether the therapist believes that the key to the door lies in identifying repressed damaging experiences from the past, faulty irrational beliefs, patterns of learned maladaptive behaviour or lack of self-actualisation. On the journey, the therapist gathers evidence that either confirms or challenges the original hypothesis. At some stage, the therapist shares this 'evidence' with the client, who either accepts or rejects it. If the client owns this discovery, both parties feel that they have stumbled on something 'real' that was waiting there, hidden but discoverable. They feel that they have created a 'common vantage point from which to survey the world together' (Taylor, 1985). Russell (1989: 505) describes this as a 'public space in which the character of social/physical realities are crafted and essayed linguistically'. The newly acquired knowledge will hopefully prove valuable to the client in understanding and changing the problem situation.

Figure 2.1 highlights many of the key qualities of a form of constructionism that focuses on the social context of language. These qualities are as follows:

- Constructionism gives precedence to the client's perceptions and experiences, rather than to 'the facts'.
- It utilises the multiplicity of narratives that clients could choose in order to bring about the changes that they want.

Attributes of social constructionism (SC)	Non-attributes
SC provides a conceptual context for understanding the counselling relationship	SC is not a new type of therapy or even a set of therapeutic techniques
SC deals with theory, personal other accounts and other evidence in terms of its usefulness rather than in terms of truth or external validity	SC is not a licence to say that all views are equally legitimate or persuasive
SC recognises that individuals will have preferences for particular ways of viewing experiences and so on	SC does not accept that these personal choices constitute truth or reality statements
SC proposes that personal knowledge derives from participation in social interaction via participation in conversation and social exchange, and holds that problems are generated by and embedded in current patterns of meaning and interaction rather than being products of inside (the individual) or outside factors	SC is not a restriction requiring that the counsellor does not hold a view, nor that references to social structures, social 'realities' and individual characteristics cannot be made
SC proposes that instructive interaction cannot have a certain outcome – that is, what the 'expert' tells the 'non-expert' does not determine what the non-expert then comes to believe, know or do	SC does not require that the counsellor can never assume an expert role or relationship with the client
SC supports the view that counselling is constructive rather than remedial	SC is not consistent with a view that counselling repairs faulty people or social systems
SC is dependent on the ability and willingness of the counsellor to remain non-attached to rules, structures and personal preferences in order to be free to consider and propose other ways of describing what appears to be happening	SC does not require that the counsellor remains personally neutral or passive to the information received
SC seeks to understand the concepts, rules and structures of the client's experiences and story	SC is not preoccupied with the construction of explanatory or causal schema
Understanding is always interpretative as SC insists that there is no privileged standpoint for understanding	SC is not simply a reframing of people's accounts with 'superior' versions

Figure 2.1   *Social Constructionism (Street and Downey, 1996: 121, reprinted with permission)*

- It emphasises the importance of 'joining with' the client in order to cocreate a new and empowering narrative.
- It invites the therapist to affirm the expertise and unique experience of the client and disown a privileged position of knowledge and power.
- It affirms the therapist's knowledge and skills in conducting conversations that create therapeutic spaces for the client.
- It pays attention to the context in which the client's narrative developed. This increases its potential for respecting and working with difference.
- It acknowledges the competence and strengths of people.
- It demands that the counsellor develop a clear sense of her own values, blind spots and biases.

Problem-focused approaches tend to do the following:

- Assume a necessary connection between a problem and its solution and that the solution should look like the problem. If, for example, the client has had a problem for a long time, it is commonly thought that it will take a long time to find and implement a solution. If the problem is complicated, then it is assumed that the solution will also need to be complicated. The solution-focused position challenges this by claiming that clients can change without in-depth analysis of their problems and that the solution construction process is separate from the problem-exploration process.
- Privilege the search for causal connections. In the psychological realm, these connections are frequently tenuous and unprovable. There may be many associated factors that contribute to the development of a problem but to settle on one and for that to determine the course of treatment is often misguided and unhelpful. Is a client depressed because he has a genetic predisposition towards depression and/or because his family life was disrupted when his parents split up when he was ten and/or he lacked the social skills and confidence to make close relationships and/or he has low self-esteem and/or he is long-term unemployed? How are we to weigh up those factors? How do we know how significant they are? How do we know when we have gone 'deep' enough? Where does the therapist start to work on an agenda as diffuse as this? How long is it going to take for change to take place? What a priori values and principles determine the line of enquiry to which the therapist will give precedence? As Segal (1986) states in his discussion of the work of Von Foerster, we are obsessed with efficient causality, a form of explanation in which the cause precedes the effect. There are other forms of causality SFT attaches greater importance to final causality, where the effect precedes the cause. This focuses attention on how our future goals shape what we do in the present. Clarity about our preferred future motivates us to do what is needed in the

present. A driver planning a journey works back from the time he wants to arrive at his destination when plotting the course, speed, amount of fuel and stopping-off places along the way. The end point determines the means. In engineering, manufacturers examine and dismantle their competitor's product, such as a car engine, in order to work out how it was made. In solution-focused therapy, the therapists facilitate clients' hopes of the desired end 'product', then help them to work back to find out how they might get there. Instead of clients trying to analyse why they've got the life they have, they redirect their energy to create the life they want.

- Require clients to undergo certain stages or events in therapy before their attempts to change will be legitimated. For example, some therapies stipulate that a client must have a cathartic experience in which deep, previously unexpressed emotions are brought to the surface. Similarly, some therapies hold that clients must achieve insight into themselves if their apparent progress is to be anything more than just a superficial fix. There is an assumption that the 'deeper' the investigation of the psyche, the more 'truthful' the findings. However there are many clients who apparently achieve insight into themselves yet remain none the wiser about how to bring about change. Some suffer from 'paralysis by analysis'. It can happen that insight proves unhelpful when it induces a fatalism born of a conviction that the past has unalterably determined the future.

In problem-focused work, the therapist uses a psychological map to explore the client's problematic terrain. As the client explores this territory she becomes aware of the obstacles in her path and, hopefully, also learns how to overcome them. In this scenario, the therapist occupies the role of an expert guide who knows the signposts and short cuts. Which route they choose depends on the kind of journey that the two parties are willing to embark on. In long-term work, they may choose the scenic route; in short-term work, the fastest and most direct.

The solution-focused therapist also has a navigational system, but clients' map-reading skills and self-knowledge of their interior and exterior landscape are the crucial directions for the journey. In keeping with his role as a 'travel companion' the therapist resists adopting professional jargon, which disempowers the client. Instead he takes a 'not knowing' position, from which he disowns the role of expert or 'the keeper of the truth' in the client's life. Together, they collaborate to negotiate a meaning for the client's experience. The purpose of their dialogue is to negotiate a meaning for the client's situation that will open up possibilities of change. For the social constructionist, language constructs and deconstructs our changing realities.

Negotiating narratives with clients is the essence of any type of therapy. For the solution-focused practitioner, certain types of narrative are more likely to motivate and support a client towards change than others. These are future-focused, competence-based and client-centred narratives. Future-focused narratives challenge beliefs that the future will be the same as the past. This is not to say that the past is not useful – it helps us to learn from mistakes and successes. When driving a car it is essential to look in the rear-view mirror occasionally, but it is advisable to spend most of the time looking through the front windscreen!

The Mental Research Institute (MRI) model

Every wrong attempt discarded is another step forward. I have not failed 10,000 times, I have successfully found 10,000 ways that will not work.

Thomas Edison

The MRI brief therapy problem-focused model claims that problems emerge because people take action to solve a problem and the actions themselves become part of the problem. These actions include under-reacting to the problem by avoiding or denying it or adopting strategies that either have little positive effect or even compound the problem. In this view, the problem is the sum of the client's failed solutions.

Practitioners from the MRI school (Weakland and Jordan, 1992: 245) describe clearly how clients repeat failed solutions.

- The client uses more of the same type of 'solution' and only varies the performance slightly by, for example, turning up the volume or increasing the frequency.
- The client avoids doing something that needs to be done. The client may not be able to summon up the energy or effort to do what she knows needs to be done.
- Clients act in ways that are irrelevant or inappropriate to the problem – the 'moving deck chairs on the Titanic' syndrome. They may engage in strategies such as overworking in order to prevent them from having to think about the problem.
- The client tries to move in two directions at the same time, in desperation choosing solutions that cancel each other out – for example, fasting and bingeing.
- The client keeps looking for the perfect solution: 'Attempts to do the impossible in actuality will prevent doing what is possible and desirable, and will also make what might otherwise be bearable appear intolerable because it is imperfect.'

Using this model demands that the therapist identify and explores the vicious circles that surround the problem and find ways for the client to interrupt the problem cycle. It is important to clarify precisely why the client has come for therapy and what exactly she hopes to gain from it.

This, as any practitioner will know, is not always easy as clients can be vague and unsure about the nature of the problem and ambivalent about what they hope to achieve from therapy. The therapist also tries to discover what the client or other significant people are doing to maintain the problem. Clients are encouraged to set clear, specific, small, but realistic, goals. The aim of these strategies is to displace the failed or attempted solution by either disrupting the status quo and/or by encouraging a quite different way of looking at or acting on the problem. Clients are usually given tasks to perform between sessions.

The focus of the work is on clients' presenting problems, not on underlying issues: 'The presenting problem offers, in one package, what the patient is ready to work on, a concentrated manifestation of whatever is wrong, and a concrete index of any progress made' (Weakland, Fisch, Watzlawick and Bodin, 1974: 147).

Both the MRI and the SFT models were influenced by the innovatory work of Milton Erickson, 'the father of strategic therapy'. According to Lankton (1990), the characteristics of Erickson's therapy were:

- *a non-pathology model* problems result from a limited repertoire of behaviour and attitudes on the part of clients
- *indirection* the therapist helps clients to tap into resources of which they were unaware, without the role of the therapist interfering
- *utilisation* this consists of mobilising any aspect of the client's experience that could usefully contribute to resolving the problem
- *action* the therapist expects clients to act outside the therapy sessions to make the changes they want
- *strategic* the therapist designs interventions specifically for each client
- *future-orientated* the emphasis is on the future, more than on the past or present
- *enchantment* the therapy seeks to engage clients in ways that appear attractive to them.

Most of these principles are found in SFT, although therapist-designed strategic interventions are rarely used. Instead, the therapist trusts the client's best instincts and sees the client as creative, imaginative and resourceful. The therapist, too, is optimistic, hopeful, creative and imaginative. He helps the client to keep going in the direction of his goals, but is not the expert who knows or chooses what that direction should be.

The epistemological basis of SFT offers the therapist rich and varied access to the client's world. Its sensitivity to the power of language in socially constructing the problem creates many possible therapeutic conversations. Its acknowledgement of the presence of many different 'truths' and standpoints validates the worldview of clients, while providing a basis for 're-authoring' (White, 1995) the client's narrative. Its recognition of the social context of language highlights the powerful impact of culture, race and gender discourses in therapy. It offers a model of the therapist–client relationship, characterised by respect for the client's expertise. Its reluctance to reify problems into fixed and defined 'truths' about clients highlights the dynamic process of change and increases the possibility of change.

Practice points

- Solutions fit the clients, not the problem.
- Sometimes it helps to know as little as possible about your clients before you meet them. There are exceptions to this.
- Exploring failed solutions can be a useful starting point.
- You can help clients without identifying the 'causes' of their problems.
- Consider how it would affect your work if you believed that 'truth was not there to be discovered, but to be invented.'
- There are power implications in taking a therapeutic stance based on social constructionism. We need to think about how it affects relationships with clients.

3

Overview of the Model

There's nothing wrong with you that what's right with you can't fix.

Baruch Shalem

The solution-focused approach has been used with a wide range of client groups and in many different settings: mental illness (Wilgosh, 1993; Dodd, 2003; Hawkes, 2003), substance misuse (Berg and Miller, 1992; Hanton, 2003), domestic violence (Lipchik, 1991), sexual abuse (Dolan, 1991; Turnell and Edwards, 1999; Darmody, 2003), couples counselling (Hudson and O'Hanlon, 1991; Iveson, 2003), parenting and school difficulties (Durrant, 1993b; Lethem, 1994; Rhodes and Ajmal, 1995; Sharry, 2003), business (Jackson and McKergow, 2002). The Brief Family Therapy Center (BFTC) in Milwaukee, USA where solution-focused therapy (SFT) originated was, and still is, a non-profit-making service for clients from socially deprived neighbourhoods. It could be argued that SFT, with its respect for clients' strengths and its down-to-earth language, is more user-friendly to people in lower socio-economic groups than many other types of therapy.

Although SFT is designed to be brief, and in practice often is, this need not always be the case. It is not time-limited in the sense of therapists offering contracts for a fixed number of sessions. De Shazer (1996) reports that, on average, clients at the BFTC attend for three sessions. Cade and O'Hanlon (1993) state that therapy should end as soon as is respectfully possible. As Miller (1994) points out, SFT cannot claim to be briefer than other methods as research has consistently shown that clients, on average, attend for four to six sessions (Koss and Butcher, 1986), regardless of the model employed. However, as we have seen, there are certain principles and methods that are more likely to make therapy brief than if others are used.

SFT adopts the principle of minimal intervention. Following Occam's axiom that 'it is vain to do with more what can be achieved with fewer', SFT makes the fewest assumptions necessary to explain the client's situation (Cade and O'Hanlon, 1993). Cade and O'Hanlon (1993: 5) argue that the analysis of ideas and repetitive sequences surrounding 'symptoms' is a sufficient level of explanation for engaging in therapy:

> Brief Therapy is primarily concerned with observable phenomena, is pragmatic and believes that problems are produced and maintained by the constructs through which difficulties are viewed and by repetitive behavioural sequences surrounding them, including the constructs and inputs of therapists.

Further, they suggest that minimal interference reduces the dangers of unduly prolonging therapy and thereby creating a sense of dependency in clients. As well as helping to keep therapy brief while respecting the uniqueness of each client, minimal theoretical assumptions discourage classifying, categorising or speculating about the problem. A feature of the minimal intervention approach is the reluctance of the solution-focused therapist to take a case history in the orthodox sense, or to formulate an explanation for the client's difficulties. Fisch (1994) suggests that the more explanatory data sought ('Why … ?' questions), as distinct from descriptive data ('What did you do next?'), the more prolonged therapy is likely to be. Explanatory data encourage elaboration by both therapist and client into speculative discourse ('I think he's been like this since I started going out to work, but on the other hand he was having a lot of problems when his father left us'). Another reason why therapy is more likely to be brief is that the therapist focuses on the problem brought by the client and does not stray into other areas of the client's life. The solution-focused therapist does not regard therapy as a definitive, once-in-a-lifetime experience, but as a supportive event that enables the client to initiate a process of ongoing change.

Problem-focused v. solution-focused

On the training courses that I run I give the participants an exercise in which they interview one another, first using a problem-focused script and then a solution-focused one. They find the contrast striking. Some of their comments include:

> The problem-focused script talks you into your problem, the solution-focused one talks you out of it.

> Asking questions about the problem makes me as the interviewer feel in control. When we talked about the client's solutions I felt she had more of the power.

> We noticed that when I asked about the problem the client felt that I had misunderstood what the problem was or that I had distorted what she had said.

> Solution talk energised us.

> We realised that the more you talked about something, whether it was the problem or a solution, the bigger it got.

> We felt that solutions were not as divisive as the problem. There is more conflict in arguing about what the problem is.

> We found that the distinction between the problem and the solution dissolved. What seemed like a problem to begin with seemed to change into a solution!

Figure 3.1 compares a problem-focused and a solution-focused approach. The therapist is not likely to verbalise all these questions – some are assumptions that guide the process. The chart is an oversimplification but it helps to highlight some key differences.

Problem-focused	Solution-focused
• How can I help you?	• How will you know that coming here today has been helpful?
• Could you tell me about the problem?	• What would you like to change?
• Is the problem a symptom of an underlying issue?	• Can we dig deep to discover solutions?
• Can you tell me more about the problem?	• Can we discover exceptions to the problem?
• How are we to understand the problem in the light of the past?	• What will the future look like without the problem?
• What defence mechanisms are operating?	• How can we use the skills and strengths of the client?
• How many sessions will we need?	• Have we achieved enough to end?

Figure 3.1   *A comparison between a problem-focused and a solution-focused approach*

How can I help you? v. How will you know that coming here today has been helpful?
Opening gambits are crucial because they reveal how the practitioner sees the change process. The first question stresses the expert role, the 'privileged position' of the interviewer, and implies that she can provide something that the client cannot give or do for himself. The second question invites the client to consider what he hopes to achieve and how he will know that he has achieved it. As far as possible, the client describes the end at the beginning. When clients have a picture of the specific outcomes they want, the focus of the work becomes clear. Instead of being the recipient of help, the client becomes an equal partner in a joint enterprise with the therapist. Figure 3.2 suggests some opening questions:

- What are your best hopes for this session?
- How will you know that coming here today has been worthwhile?
- How do you know that now is a good time to make changes?
- How many times do you think we will need to meet?
- How will you know when things are beginning to get better for you?

Figure 3.2   *Goal-orientated questions*

Could you tell me about the problem? v. What
would you like to change?

Kelly (1955) said, 'if you do not know what is wrong with a person, ask him; he may tell you'. This is a useful reminder of the importance of the client's construction of the problem and a warning against the imposition of a problem/solution frame by the therapist. A problem-focused approach gathers as much information as possible about the patterns of the client's problem behaviour in order to design an intervention to break the problematic vicious circle. There is an argument that goes, the more you know about what is going wrong in a client's life the more that makes you an expert in failure. Clients and counsellors can become skilled in constructing such a complicated edifice around the problem that they can't see solutions for the scaffolding! For some clients problem-talk is well rehearsed and delivered on automatic pilot. When they move into solution-talk there is a greater sense of being on new territory, of being 'more real', more in the moment. Solution-talk can be hard work for the client and the counsellor.

A solution-focused approach will spend less time on the client's problem-past and more on obtaining a description of the kind of future the client wants. The question above, invites the client to describe the specific behaviour he wants to alter and sets a climate of expectancy about change. It enquires what it is he is motivated to change and implies that he has the power to make changes.

Is the problem a symptom of an underlying issue?
v. Can we dig deep to discover solutions?

The first question implies a structural use of language, as described in Chapter 2, and sets the therapist on the quest for the meaning behind the client's story. It may not be immediately clear to the client that the therapist has made a decision that will determine the nature and parameters of the ensuing conversation. The second question would not be asked openly, but is, rather, an assumption made by the therapist – namely, that underneath the surface the client is using many different strategies to cope with life and that many other strategies have either become buried under the weight of a problem-history or lie untapped. The iceberg metaphor, used so often in therapy, can refer to solutions as well as problems! In some ways the solution-focused approach could be summed up as a process of bringing solutions to the surface. Clients not only want to get their problems off their chests, they often want to get their solutions off their chests, too. An interviewer, preoccupied with assessment and analysis, can miss what is in front of her face.

Can you tell me more about the problem? v. Can
we discover exceptions to the problem?

The first question invites 'problem talk'. The client provides evidence for the behaviour, thoughts and feelings that he, or someone else, regards as problematic. As the therapist listens, she seeks elaboration of the problem by reflecting, questioning or summarising the narrative in order to formulate an understanding or identify a pattern. As she listens to the content of the narrative, she will also attend to the verbal and non-verbal ways in which the client delivers it. Clients can often present with chaotic, negative versions of their lives and want to recruit us into it. We can pick up their hopelessness and confusion and begin to feel overwhelmed by the extent of the problem.

The second question invites the client to describe times when the problem does not happen. These are episodes when the client is controlling or resisting the problem. For the solution-focused therapist, the seeds of solutions lie in these exceptional, non-problematic times and it is about these times that she will be most curious. Perhaps it is unsurprising to find that clients talk about their solutions differently from the way they talk about their problems. Most people like to talk about successes and actually enjoy receiving credit for what they have achieved. Recognition of success breeds confidence, which in turn generates further success. It is often the case that clients only begin to acknowledge their own solutions when someone else has validated them.

How are we to understand the problem in the light of the past?
v. What will the future look like without the problem?
The former implies that the 'truth' about the problem lies in understanding the past and that the solution to the problem is intrinsically connected to the past and present experiences of the client. It also focuses attention on finding causes in order to explain current behaviour. Popular conceptions of therapy lead many clients to believe that the primary purpose of therapy is to identify the unconscious origins of their behaviour. They expect that therapy will be a long, intrusive and painful experience. This expectation must deter many people from seeking help.

The second question focuses attention on the client's picture of the future. This glimpse into the future is a powerful factor in explaining the client's current behaviour and also suggests the direction in which he hopes therapy might take him. One of the key characteristics of the solution-focused approach is that it detaches the search for solutions from the analysis of problems. Jackson and McKergow (2002) give a good example of this when they describe the phenomenon of 'phantom traffic jams'. We are all familiar with motorway jams that seem to have no immediate cause – no accidents or roadworks. Apparently their cause is that one or more cars change lanes suddenly and cause other drivers to brake quickly. This chain reaction eventually leads to cars further back coming to a complete stop. The solution to the problem lies in slowing down all the traffic so that it keeps moving at a reasonable speed but is not disrupted if someone changes lane suddenly. The point being made here is that the solution emerged not so much from studying the problem episodes, but from studies of times when traffic flowed smoothly.

What defence mechanisms are operating? v. How can we use the skills and strengths of the client?
These questions or assumptions reveal the working models adopted by different therapists. The first assumes that clients' behaviour is various unconscious strategies to defend their threatened egos. One of these defences is resistance – clinically understood as the client rejecting insights put forward by the therapist. For the solution-focused worker, resistance is a defence adopted by the client to signal that the style or pace of the relationship is not helpful.

The second question emphasises that anything the client brings to the relationship can be useful – values, resources, failures, networks, dreams and preferences. In training solution-focused workers we use the 'Big I' exercise, which draws out, by means of questions, many different facets of the client – for example, their preferences in food, music, clothes, leisure, exercise and so on. All these add up to the 'big I' of someone's identity. This identity goes beyond those aspects of the client's life that are problematic and it is probably in the process of exploring those other features that the problems can be overcome. Solution-focused workers will not describe their clients as 'damaged' but, if they did, it would be to highlight that they can be 'healthy' in other parts of their lives.

How many sessions will we need? v. Have we achieved enough to end?
In some models of therapy it is the therapist who unilaterally decides the length of the course of treatment. An initial contract will stipulate a specific number of sessions with a review after, for example, in brief therapy, six sessions. This is not the solution-focused way. Instead, the therapist consults the client to find out how many sessions he thinks he needs. Some clients will have clear ideas about this, but many will not. After the first session she may also tactfully raise the question as to whether or not the client found it helpful and how he feels about needing further sessions. This can be done without giving the impression to clients that their problems are minor and do not entitle them to further help. During the course of the work – however long it is – there will be an ongoing dialogue between the two parties to ensure that they are addressing the right agenda and that the sessions are helpful. Clients will be invited to ask themselves, 'What needs to happen so that you know you don't need to come here any longer?'

Assumptions

The solution-focused approach, therefore, makes a number of pragmatic assumptions.

- Problems are part of life – overcoming them is what makes us human.
- Problems are embedded in language and change may involve deconstructing the language around the problem.
- Problems take place in the interaction between the person and his social environment. Problems are not 'inside' someone.
- Understanding a problem does not have to precede solving it – the understanding can emerge later, if at all.
- People are resilient, creative problem-solvers.
- People often do not remember or learn from times when they use 'solutions'.
- People engage more with an approach that builds on their strengths than with one that highlights their deficiencies.
- They are more likely to implement customised strategies than formulaic 'one size fits all' solutions.
- It is more effective to build on 'what works', than to get someone to do something for the first time.
- Small steps forward tend to be more helpful than big plans.

These assumptions have important consequences throughout the helping process.

Contracting and assessment

Contracting
The aim of the contract made between the therapist and the client is to establish a clear and agreed basis for the work. Clients approach therapists with a wide range of expectations as to what might happen and what their respective roles might be. Their own and other people's experience of seeking help; the degree to which they are coming of their own free will; their level of distress; and their perceptions of social attitudes towards their problem will all shape their expectations and how wary or suspicious they may be. In each case the therapist needs to find out what the client wants and whether or not therapy is the right form of help.

It is crucially important to listen carefully to the client's opening conversation, as he will be acutely sensitive to the first response the therapist makes. If he does not feel heard and accepted, he may withdraw cooperation, sabotage attempts at solution-talk or simply not come back again.

In the early stages of contracting it is important to move at the client's pace. Brief does not mean rushed; pressurising the client is counterproductive and disrespectful. The solution-focused therapist aims to develop a cooperative 'joining' with the client in a warm, positive, accepting relationship that includes the adoption of a 'one down' (non-expert) position in which the client teaches the therapist about his view of the world and how the therapist could co-operate with him. Consumers want their preferences and priorities to be taken seriously by providers. Joining with the client involves matching the client's language, offering positive feedback and a willingness to adapt one's interviewing style to suit the client. The therapist treats the client as the expert in his own life, while the therapist has expertise in creating a therapeutic environment. The structure of the therapy depends on a number of factors:

* agency policy, which dictates the maximum number of sessions, length and possibly frequency
* the terms of specific contracts that demand the client be seen quickly
* the attitude of the therapist towards brief therapy and its effectiveness – it is crucial that the therapist believes in what she is doing as, if she regards brief therapy as second best and unlikely to produce lasting change, then she will fail to communicate the expectancy required for its effectiveness.

Most solution-focused therapists who are free to do so avoid contracting for a set number of sessions. This is in the belief that it is possible to slow down the client's rate of progress by prescribing in advance the number of sessions required. Some clients might feel after one or two sessions that sufficient change has taken place. Committing both parties to six or more sessions, for example, runs the risk of the work expanding to fill the time available and thus losing its momentum and focus. It is more common to ask the client at the end of the first session whether or not he felt it had been helpful to talk and if he would like to meet the therapist again and, if so, when. Encouraging the client to take time to think about this helps to ensure that the client retains choice and power over the work. This devolving of power to the client might not suit everyone. Some clients might feel more secure and confident in feeling that the therapist knows how many sessions are necessary and that they can plan their lives more easily around a structured course. In time-limited contracts, some clients will feel unsure about raising big issues, as they will worry about whether or not there is enough time to explore them properly. Many people need reassuring that they have an entitlement to the time they need and that they are not wasting the therapist's time.

The frequency of meetings is also a subject of negotiation – there being no set rule about weekly meetings. The therapist tries to fit in as far as possible with the pattern that most suits the individual client. Imposing a schedule on clients increases the risk that they will drop out prematurely. In addition to the fact that weekly attendance can pose serious practical problems for many clients, a longer interval between sessions can provide them with more opportunities to develop their problem-solving strategies. However, setting intervals too far apart can destroy the focused intensity and momentum needed. Some models of brief therapy advocate that the client keeps a session or number of sessions 'in the bank' to be drawn on, either after a stipulated period of time or when a difficulty arises. Another option is to hold weekly sessions for the first two or three weeks in order to build a sense of momentum, then meet at two weekly or monthly intervals thereafter. Clients have different attitudes towards the amount of time that they are able or willing to devote to resolving their problems. This ranges from a wish for a 'fast fix' to a belief that only long-term work will be effective. These expectations will require addressing – both may find it helpful to see small signs of progress early on.

With regard to the length of sessions, there is nothing sacrosanct about the 50-minute hour. Concentrating for that length of time is difficult for many people, including the therapists. There are situations that demand that amount of time and more, but there are also many occasions when it would be more therapeutic to end the session earlier – for example, when the client has made a decision or come to a point of resolution. It is better to end on a strong, positive note than prolong the session unduly.

Assessment

Some SFT practitioners do not screen clients for suitability, preferring to work with whoever comes or is referred to them. Their rationale is that there are no clear predictive signs to indicate or contraindicate a particular client's ability to engage in and gain from SFT. In SFT there is no clear distinction between assessment and intervention. Interventions start even before the therapist meets the client. Some forms of assessment run counter to the spirit and constructionist philosophy of SFT in that they emphasise deficits, pathology, crises, failure and trauma. There is insufficient recognition of the coping strategies, the strength of character, the courage and the stamina that the client has needed to cope to date. Recurring detailed assessments of this kind can disempower the client and are anti-therapeutic. In the initial stages of an SFT first session, the therapist seeks to discover what the client perceived as helpful or unhelpful in previous helping relationships. This provides the therapist with important information on how to join with the client and foster cooperation.

Visitor, complainant and customer

De Shazer (1988) uses the terms 'visitor', 'complainant' and 'customer' to distinguish between clients with different agendas. From a constructionist point of view, the description belongs not so much to the client as to the constructed relationship between the two parties. A visiting relationship is one in which the client does not think he has a problem or does not want to be in therapy or both. A complainant one is where the person is willing to discuss the problem but sees the solution as lying elsewhere. A customer relationship is where the client recognises that he has a particular problem and sees the session as a vehicle for doing something about it. It is a mistake to treat these three types of relationship in the same way. On occasions, the visiting or complainant relationship can become a customer one when the two parties manage to negotiate a clear benefit that the client could gain from therapy. On other occasions a negotiated referral or an agreement to discontinue counselling might be the outcome. Fisch, Weakland and Segal (1982: 39) use the analogy of the window-shopper who slips into a shop to keep out of a heavy shower, and who has no intention of buying anything but may try to look as if she has, to describe the ambivalence many clients bring to the first session.

Figure 3.3 represents various positions clients might adopt with respect to change. They suggest that the client's attitude towards change could be quite complicated. These positions may reflect a lack of knowledge, awareness, motivation or the social skills to move the problem forward. In helping the client to change, the therapist needs to meet the client where he is at the time.

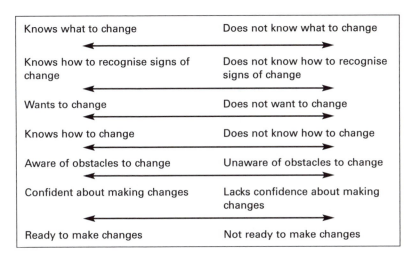

Figure 3.3   *Client positions about change*

The ideal solution-focused client might present for therapy and say: 'I am very clear what I would like to change in my life and I am willing to invest a lot of effort into making those changes. I have already begun to make progress and I would like to build on my strengths to develop those solutions. I will be clear and specific in describing what is happening in the area of my life that is causing me concern. I do not wish to explore my life story or search for hidden meanings to my life. I want to co-operate with you and put into effect any ideas we may generate about change. I will report back to you promptly on my progress. I will want to end therapy as soon as I have begun to make progress.' Unfortunately, one rarely meets such a client! However, clients who are motivated to change will probably hold some of these sentiments. In pre-session literature clients will be informed what the work entails and will be able to make an informed choice about their participation.

Focal issue

Most forms of brief therapy stress the importance of having a focal or central issue for the work. The clearer and more specific the agenda, the greater the likelihood that the therapy will be purposeful and effective. In SFT the focus of the work is the issue presented by the client. Barret-Kruse (1994) describes the presenting problem as 'a gift to the therapist'. The framing of the problem and the solution are matters for negotiation. The closer the therapist can keep to the client's agenda, the more likely it is that the client will feel motivated to change. By tracking the client's agenda, the therapist develops an empathic and collaborative relationship. The agenda has to be specific, clear and concrete in its formulation, with minimal opportunities for expansion. It is not always possible to achieve this in a first session, as clients are often confused, anxious, overwhelmed and unsure how therapy can help them.

In SFT the therapist accepts what the client brings and does not speculate about underlying issues or the origins of the problem. The priority is to find a common language to describe what the client wants to change and begin to explore how those changes would affect the client's life. This sounds simple but it is often far from easy. The client's experience of therapy is more complicated than the therapist imagines.

Clients often present with multiple interlocking problems that require prioritising – not in the sense that once one problem is 'solved' attention then turns to the next on the list, but in the sense that the client agrees a single issue will be the focus of the work and other problems will only be discussed in so far as they affect the central issue. The therapist needs to find leverage – namely, a solvable problem that the client wants and is able to work on.

EXAMPLE

Therapist: So you would like to talk about the way you and your partner disagree about controlling your children. You have mentioned that there are other problems about work and health, but am I right that you want to concentrate on the disagreements with your partner and that the other matters will only come up if they throw light on that?

This agreement allows the client to introduce relevant material from other problem areas, but only in so far as it sheds light on the central issue. It also gives the therapist permission to keep the client to the point. Steenbarger (1994) concluded from his review of various studies that brief therapy is most suitable for clients who are highly aware of focal problem patterns and are able to form a working alliance. Clients who present with broad, diffuse and poorly understood patterns and who need considerable time to form a trusting alliance are more likely to need an extended period of exploratory work. In my experience, it is a great advantage when clients can articulate their problem and their goals, but it does not mean that initial vagueness and lack of clarity about the future disqualifies them from brief solution-focused work. It simply means that the therapist and the client have to work harder and may need more time.

Principles

There are a number of principles or assumptions that guide solution-focused work. These can be helpfully shared between the practitioner and the client.

If it isn't broken don't fix it

This principle is a warning to practitioners to be careful about expanding the 'problem' by looking for more and more aspects of the client's life to fix. It emphasises that people *have* problems, rather than that they *are* problems, or, to be more precise, problems happen in the relationship between the person and the social environment, they do not belong to people as if they lived in a vacuum. SFT does not see clients as being emotionally or psychologically sick (and therefore in need of a cure) or damaged (and therefore in need of repair), but as temporarily unable to overcome a life difficulty because they have not yet found a way out of or around it. Instead of focusing on pathology (the answer doesn't lie there), it seeks out and builds on what is healthy and functioning in people's lives. We can only build on strengths.

SFT encourages a period of problem-free talk with the client (George, Iveson and Ratner, 1990). This may take the form of a preliminary informal conversation (not to be confused with small talk) about what the client enjoys doing at times when the problem is not affecting him. This can often provide useful clues to the therapist when she comes to look for client strengths and to devise strategies. The therapist may disclose information about herself or the therapy that she feels would help this particular client.

Building on what is right, rather than fixing what is wrong (O'Hanlon and Weiner-Davis, 1989) also helps to limit the agenda and keep therapy brief. When clients feel overwhelmed by a problem, they tend to lose sight of their strengths and resources. Skott-Myhre (1992) outlines the following as being the basic principles of a competency-based approach:

- What people do is based on what they believe to be true about the world.

The first task of the therapist is to hear and validate the client's experience and subjective perception of the world. This subjective view may not be consistent with the 'facts' (the historical truth) but it is the client's 'truth'.

- What people believe to be true is shaped and developed by the conversations they have with each other.

People do not acquire their experience in a vacuum, but, rather, in a social context in which language describes that experience to other people. We need to know the audience for the conversation in which people engage.

- Each person is embedded in a unique dialogic ecology.

There is a mutual dialogue between the individual, other people and the social and cultural environment in which he lives. A useful tool for understanding the social context of this dialogue, based on constructionist epistemology, is discourse analysis (Widdicombe, 1993). It sets out to understand the rules that govern social intercourse and assumes that people use language to construct the world according to their own interests, rather than as a representation of an objective reality out there. It is not possible for anyone to approach the discourse of another from a position of neutrality as we all have our own filters through which we interpret the world. The issue of power is closely allied to the dominance of some forms of discourse over others – for example, white and male over black and female.

- The nature and substance of this ecology is constantly changing.

Discourse analysis contends that meanings are multiple and constantly shifting according to the audience. The language of the word games used in therapy is itself in a state of flux. It could be argued that the dominant form of therapeutic discourse to date, psychoanalysis, is giving way to more pragmatic models that do not carry the weight of ideological baggage the former collected.

- Each and every person is inherently competent and has all the resources necessary for change.
- The role of therapy is not to create change but discover where change is occurring and amplify it.

This is a key strategy in SFT – building on what the client brings and what is already making a difference to the problem.

- Therapy need not take a long time.

This belief attacks the notion that effective therapy needs to be long term. Equally, however, this does not mean that brief therapy is the right choice for every client. Some clients require long-term therapy and to offer anything less would be to cheat them of what they need.

'If it is not broken do not fix it' is a useful reminder to the overly eager practitioner who wants to problem-solve but we need to balance it with the fact that we all need to engage in maintenance, otherwise things may well get broken in time!

Small changes can lead to bigger changes
One of the characteristics of solution-focused work is the way in which it breaks down the process of change into small manageable steps. According to Rosenbaum, Hoyt and Talmon (1990) there are three advantages to such an approach:

- It takes the pressure off both therapist and client, so that neither tries too hard. Trying too hard to bring about change can itself cause problems. There are times when it is wiser to do less rather than more.
- The client is more likely to be willing to make a small change than a big one. There are always exceptions to this of course and the therapist needs to respond to the client who is ready for rapid and radical change.
- Any kind of movement may suffice to ignite hope in the client. Generating hope and confidence, providing it is not false, is an important ingredient in brief therapy. Clients, feeling overwhelmed by their problems and ambivalent about change, often find making any kind of start a daunting prospect. The SFT approach is to find a small, but significant, starting point for initiating change.

EXAMPLE

Frances feels that there is virtually no constructive communication with her partner. The starting point for change may be a particular time and event, such as the sequence of events that takes place when one partner returns home. The client may be asked: 'Who greets whom, when, how? What would happen if it were handled differently? If s/he felt welcomed home, how would that make a difference? What would you do if you were to welcome her/him home in a different way? What would need to happen for that to happen? Could you do that?'

We are changing all of the time – only the pace and direction are uncertain. The skilled therapist respects and matches the client's pace, neither holding her back, nor pressurising her to move more quickly than she wants or feels able. At times, the pace is slow and measured, at others fast and radical. Initiating change can often have repercussions beyond the focal starting point. Experiencing change can restore the person's sense of choice and control and encourage the making of further changes.

(Continued)

(Continued)

Yet, changing one element in the system, however small, does not guarantee that the consequences will be wholly helpful or constructive, at least in the short term. Changing behaviour or attitudes can bring negative effects as well, such as further oppression, punishment, sanctions, a heightened sense of how much still needs to be done or an increased sense of inadequacy. Initiating change can trigger memories of past hurts, regrets, failures or losses.

If it's working keep doing it
The therapist encourages the client to keep doing what she has shown she can already do. This constructive behaviour may have started prior to the therapy (pre-session change). Clients may need to sustain the new pattern of behaviour for some time before they feel confident about maintaining it. At first this new way of handling the problem may feel artificial and make them self-conscious. They would prefer it to feel more natural and real. However, experimenting with new behaviour is like learning your lines in a play or the notes in your music before you can really get into the part or become musical. Therapy can provide opportunities for rehearsal and experimentation.

If it's not working stop doing it
In keeping with the MRI principle of abandoning failed solutions, the solution-focused therapist encourages clients to do something different (almost anything) to break the failure cycle. This may run counter to family scripts (for the therapist and the client), such as 'if at first you don't succeed, try, try again.' It can often happen that changing the time and place in which the client 'does' the problem can break the stuck routine.

Keep therapy as simple as possible
There is a danger that the ideology of the therapist, particularly if it entails looking for hidden explanations and unconscious factors, will complicate the relationship. Solution-focused therapists advocate minimal intrusion into the client's life and look for ways of ending the relationship as soon as possible. The constructionist position dispenses with the notion that the therapist has, through her training, a privileged view of the client's problem.

Process model of solution-focused therapy

Figure 3.4 describes three main themes that emerge in solution-focused conversations and the interventions that take place under them. As with all such models, it attempts to map out the territory, it is not the territory itself. The process is not a logical, linear sequence of events. There is a flexibility that enables the therapist to respond to the individual client by weaving the dialogue between problem/solution; past/future; individual/ system; goal/strategies. Although there are standard formulae, such as the miracle question and the first session task, the process as a whole is not mechanical. There are three types of discourse that take place:

- change discourse is a therapeutic conversation that emphasises the changing experience of the client in relation to his or her ability to solve the problem
- solution discourse comprises the intermediate interventions used by the therapist to help the client bridge the gap between the current change processes and the strategies required to obtain the goals of the client
- strategy discourse is a cooperative engagement between the therapist and the client to design and monitor the implementation of realistic plans towards the achievement of the client's goals.

Change discourse	Solution discourse	Strategy discourse
problem deconstruction	acknowledge/validate problem	define solvable central problem/focus
seek competence	compliment and affirm	utilise/reinforce learning
seek exceptions	miracle question	clarify goals/identify existing and transferable solutions
set goals	scale goals	establish endings and evaluate
circular questions	identify and reframe interactional patterns	plan new interactional patterns
behavioural language	clear specific observable descriptions	deliver message give task
Therapist help is characterised by: optimism, hope, support, confidence, collaboration, empathy, competence.		

Figure 3.4   *Solution-focused process model*

Change discourse
From the very beginning of the relationship, the therapist focuses on the theme of change. She communicates a belief that change is already taking place and that she expects change to continue to take place. In SFT, this climate of change encompasses the time prior to the first session. The person with whom the client makes the appointment asks the client to

notice whether or not any changes take place between the time of making the appointment and the first session (known as pre-session change). Typically, the therapist will enquire about these changes early on in the first session.

In the ebb and flow of change discourse, the therapist paces and times the questions that form the main speech events of the discourse. Questions open therapeutic space and offer new or different ways of thinking about situations. The therapist is curious about what is already happening in the client's life. The client becomes recruited into change-orientated language. Depending on the ability of the client to engage in this way, the therapist either continues to develop the change theme or allows the client to engage in further descriptions of the problem.

The task of the therapist is to find leverage for change. The prospect of change often creates ambivalence in the client, with discourse about change typically swinging between problem and change talk and between conversations about the past, the present and the future. If the therapist unsuccessfully attempts to initiate change talk, then it is necessary to return to problem exploration until another shift becomes possible. It can happen that a client is unable to engage in change talk in any meaningful or sustained way for some time and in some cases never manages to do so. It is with such clients that a solution-focused method fails.

The principal elements in the discourse on change are as follows:

- *Competence talk* The therapist identifies and affirms strengths and qualities of the client that can be used to solve the problem (de Shazer, 1988). The coping mechanisms that have been used by the client to date are acknowledged and reinforced.
- *Exception talk* Freedman and Combs (1993: 296) describe seeking exceptions as, 'ways in which people recover experiences at odds with their dominant story. By highlighting different events, they are opening space for the authoring of new stories.' The therapist attempts to engage the client in seeking exceptions to the problem – that is, those occasions when the problem is not happening or being managed better. This includes the search for transferable solutions (Berg, 1991; de Shazer, 1994). It is also helpful to identify 'solutions' that have worked or indeed failed in the past.
- *Context-changing talk* The therapist helps to put the problem into a different frame – one that will make it more solvable (O'Hanlon and Wilk, 1987). The frame used in SET is interactional – that is, it recognises that the ways people behave and the problems they have, develop within the context of the people and the situations that surround them. The level of focus is on the observable patterns of behaviour. Change comes from redefining the situation or altering the problem patterns. Circular statements or questions are used to explore the client's network.

- *Deconstructing the problem* The discourse about change employs descriptive language. It uses the client's words to clarify the changes that are the client's goals. It avoids abstract words, such as depression, self-esteem and stress, in favour of a detailed description of the client's ordinary day-to-day behaviour. The therapist often, but not always, translates the client's feelings, attitudes or personality characteristics into observable behaviour. There is an assumption that inner thoughts and feelings usually manifest themselves in behaviour.

Solution discourse
The discourse on solutions need not succeed that on change in terms of time, but may occur simultaneously with it. The principal elements of this discourse are the following:

- *Formation of a collaborative relationship* Rapport can emerge when the client begins to sense that the therapist and he are working together and making a difference to the problem. Empathy need not be a precondition for client change, but can accompany or follow it. It is sometimes achieved as a consequence of the client attributing positive change to the helpfulness of the therapist. This collaborative stance is orientated towards client goals rather than the investigation and understanding of the problem. It consists of support, encouragement, compliments, affirmation, attention to the client's goals and active participation on the part of the therapist. There is a commitment to respecting what the client wants, providing it is not unlawful or unethical. Once the therapist has adequately understood the client's difficulties and the client feels accepted, both parties cocreate an agenda for change.
- *The miracle question* This is a key intervention, typically used in a first session, but which may also reappear in subsequent sessions. It aims to identify existing solutions and resources and clarify the client's goals in realistic terms. It is a future-orientated question designed to help the client describe, as clearly and as specifically as possible, what his life will be like once the problem has been solved or is being managed better.
- *Scaling* The primary purpose of scaling is to set client goals, measure progress and establish priorities for action. Scaling questions are also used to discover how motivated the client is towards change and how confident he is about solving the problem.
- *Reframing* By reframing, the therapist helps the client to find another way of looking at the problem – one that will hopefully increase the chances of the client overcoming the problem. In SFT the meaning of the client's experiences is negotiable, depending on the outcome of the linguistic transactions in which the client and therapist engage. The purpose of the therapeutic dialogue is to negotiate jointly a meaning to the client's situation that will create the possibility of change for him.

Strategy discourse
This consists partly of identifying existing, but until now, devalued strategies in the client's life. Again, timing and sensitivity are crucial in sensing the optimum moment for engaging the client in a discourse about strategy. The interruption of old patterns, even if they were clearly failing, and the adoption of new patterns, raises fears, doubts and anxieties in most clients. The issue of ownership of strategies is clearly important. The following are the main elements in the discourse on strategy:

- *Utilisation*
  This is the mobilisation by the therapist of the client's experiences, values, skills, ideas and feelings in pursuit of the client's desired goal. The confidence and motivation of the client will obviously be important factors in the choice of strategies. The therapist recognises and reinforces the client's prior learning.
- *Development of solutions*
  The solution-focused method advocates incremental changes, small advances towards the goal, with the emphasis being on the client continuing to do what is already proving to be helpful. These steps emerge from both discovering exceptions to the problem and answers to the 'miracle question'. They include the abandonment of 'solutions' that have repeatedly failed in the past.
- *Clarifications of endings and evaluation*
  The client's goals are the sought-after outcomes of the therapy. The therapist explores with the client how these can be achieved and in which order of priority. During and after each session, the therapist evaluates with the client whether or not what they are doing together is proving helpful.
- *The message and task giving*
  This is the concluding stage in each session. The therapist summarises the constructive strategies described by the client in the session and reinforces and compliments progress. In most cases she will give the client a specific task to carry out before the next session.

Practice points

- 'It is vain to do with more what can be achieved with fewer' (Occam).
- If in doubt, ask the client.
- Assessment is an intervention.
- If it works for the client, encourage him or her to keep doing it.
- The first step in a long journey may be to take the stone out of your shoe.
- Work with whatever the client brings.

4

The First Session

Therapy is often a matter of tipping the first domino.

Milton Erickson, cited in Rossi (1980)

Aims of the first session

In the first session the solution-focused practitioner seeks to:

- form a collaborative relationship with the client
- create a climate for change
- clarify as far as possible the client's goals
- highlight the client's resources
- negotiate tasks.

Written accounts of counselling fail to capture the intangibles of the therapeutic relationship. Transcripts of solution-focused sessions can look slick and mechanical and devoid of mystery. It needs to be reiterated that the quality of our relationships with clients as human beings is more significant than any techniques or theories we use or hold. Technique is no substitute for a relationship built on respectful and attentive listening, reflective silences, empathy, genuineness, immediacy and acceptance. One element of this is for the practitioner to be transparent in using the approach and to ensure that his clients receive accessible information about the approach, so that they know what to expect and what will be expected of them.

Forming a collaborative relationship

All clients come for help with expectations, some of which can be problematic, some extremely helpful.

- They may have had previous negative experiences of seeking help. This requires exploration so that lessons can be learnt on both sides. It is a sign of respect for the client when the counsellor adapts his style in the light of this knowledge. Clients can also share their positive experiences of previous help and again this is immensely helpful to the counsellor in knowing how he can best collaborate. To adapt an educational axiom, 'If they don't change the way you help them, then help them the way they change.'

- They may hold fixed ideas about what should happen. Clients who have visited counsellors or advisers or read self-help books may hold views about how clients and counsellors should behave. Practitioners of the solution-focused approach may well not fit their stereotype. Their interest in clients' strengths and successes may come as a surprise to clients who expect to talk at length about their problems, their failures, their complexes and weaknesses. They may find this shift in emphasis hard to take, particularly if they believe that problem analysis is essential for the counselling to be effective.

The solution-focused counsellor first listens attentively and empathically to the client's concerns. Solution-focused literature (especially in the early years) rarely alluded to the quality of the therapeutic relationship. Empathy did not feature in the indexes of the key texts. Similarly, there was little discussion about the part played by the personality of the counsellor. To this day, the solution-focused community does not demand that those members working as therapists undergo therapy themselves as an integral part of their training. This is a bone of contention between solution-focused therapists and various therapy bodies, which demand personal therapy of its members before granting them accreditation.

De Shazer (1996) stated that he assumed empathy when working with clients, but was reluctant to use the word or define it. O'Hanlon and Beadle (1994) do not use the term, but, rather, their own phrase – 'validating and acknowledging the client's experience' – which seems to be very close to the conventional meaning of empathy. However the concept of empathy itself is not as simple as first appears. Bachelor (1988) in a study of empathy found that 44 per cent of clients perceived their counsellor's empathy to be cognitive in nature, 30 per cent as affective, 18 per cent as sharing and 7 per cent as nurturant. She concluded that empathy had different meanings for different clients and counsellors should not consider it to be a universal construct. Duncan (1992: 21) described empathy as:

> attitudes and behaviours that place the client's perceptions and experiences above theoretical content and personal values; empathy is operationalised by therapist attempts not only to accept the internal frame of reference of the client, but more importantly to work within the expressed meaning system of the client.

This is very similar to de Shazer's (1994) term 'reader-focused', which he uses to describe a person-centred approach to the client's narrative, in contrast to a 'text-focused' approach.

The solution-focused counsellor uses empathy to form a therapeutic alliance, although he is unlikely to reflect feelings back to the client as often as in a person-centred approach. There is no belief that expressing feelings is the essence of the counselling itself. The solution-focused counsellor aims to take a respectful collaborative stance orientated towards client goals. It is implied that empathic rapport will emerge when the client senses that she and the counsellor are working together in making a difference. From this perspective, empathy is not a precondition for client change, but accompanies or follows it. It is sometimes achieved when the client sees progress and links it with the work done with the counsellor. Empathy is a quality of the therapeutic relationship. It emerges from the understanding, warmth and acceptance shown by the counsellor. It is demonstrated in respectful attention to the client's goals. Respecting and joining with the client's goals is a core solution-focused value (of course this is not possible when the clients' goals are illegal or unethical). This sense of client-centred collaboration drives the agenda for change.

Creating a climate for change

People rarely seek help with an absolute commitment to change. They are much more likely to be ambivalent, anxious that they be allowed *not* to change, as well as to change what is necessary. The purpose of counselling, however, is to bring about the changes that the client is willing to invest effort in achieving. Inevitably there will be a need to start or stop certain behaviour. For the constructionist, there are no 'things' to be changed, such as one's personality, but there are multiple choices facing the client. Assuming that the current situation is one the client does not want, she needs to reframe the problem or seek solutions.

From the outset, the counsellor engages the client in a therapeutic conversation about the client's changing perceptions and experience of the problem with the aim of increasing the client's understanding. This differs from the exploratory stage in some other therapies, the purpose of which is to gather information from the client so that the counsellor can formulate a working hypothesis about the problem. As the client begins to articulate her problems, the solution-focused counsellor acknowledges and validates her concerns and feelings while paying particular attention to her strengths, skills and coping strategies.

Pre-session change
The solution-focused approach assumes that change is inevitable and the scene is set for this by an intervention known as pre-session change.

When making an appointment, the counsellor, or the contact person in the agency, asks the client to notice any changes that take place between the time of making the appointment and the first session. When the client comes for the first session the counsellor will enquire about these changes. In the past, counsellors often ignored or even denied that clients had begun to solve their problems prior to engaging in counselling. Some practitioners dismissed client-reported change as illusory, temporary or as denial and a 'flight into health' in order to avoid facing the 'real' problems.

Weiner-Davis, de Shazer and Gingerich (1987) explored the phenomenon of pre-session change and discovered that, of 30 parents with family problems, 20 (66 per cent) reported positive pre-session changes. The researchers claim that, in addition to the 20 who reported positive changes, the remainder often recalled pre-treatment changes later in the session. Lawson (1994), in replicating this research, interviewed 82 clients. Of these 51 (62 per cent) reported having observed positive pre-session change, whereas the remaining 31 (37.8 per cent) reported either no change (28 per cent) or that things seemed worse (3 per cent).

Positive pre-session change is empowering for the client because the changes have taken place independently of the counsellor and, therefore, the credit belongs solely to the client. By granting recognition to pre-session change, the counsellor can help the client to build on what he has already begun to do. Pre-session change can reveal clients' strategies, beliefs, values and skills that will be helpful in constructing solutions. This 'flying start' helps to accelerate the process of change and increases the likelihood of the work being brief.

Clients are often pleasantly surprised when the counsellor acknowledges the efforts and progress that they have made. They may have come into counselling feeling vulnerable, embarrassed, ashamed or a failure. They may expect criticism, blame or even humiliation, as this has been the reaction of others. Instead they experience respect for their struggles and a genuine celebration of their achievements.

This is an emotional event for many clients. Feeling that the counsellor understands how hard it has been for them to cope is deeply affirming and transforming. It injects hope and optimism that things will continue to move in the right direction. Sometimes making the first move is the hardest part. This can be particularly the case when the counsellor is of a different age group, gender or race from the client.

EXAMPLE

Counsellor: Have you noticed any differences since you contacted us last week?
Client: When I phoned you I was at rock bottom. I just couldn't stop crying. I couldn't eat, sleep or go out. I still feel pretty awful, but I'm not crying so much.
Counsellor: So what helped?
Client: My friends have been very supportive. They have made sure I've not been on my own.
Counsellor: So it's felt better having someone with you most of the time.
Client: I don't know what I would have done without them.
Counsellor: Has anything else helped?

Client:	I told myself life had to go on. There's nothing I can do about it.
Counsellor:	You feel you have to make the best of it and somehow get on with things.
Client:	I know it's going to take time to get used to it.
Counsellor:	Has anything else helped?
Client:	For the first couple of days I drank quite a lot and I felt terrible when I woke up in the morning.
Counsellor:	So you've found that drinking too much doesn't help.
Client:	Yes.

In the above example the client sees a clear connection between steps she has taken and the resolution of her problems, but sometimes clients do not see improvements as significant. Perhaps under the influence of other key people in their lives they devalue progress as marginal, accidental or exceptional. A solution-focused practitioner will not be deflected by such answers. It is often the case that clients who initially disown progress come to see that they have made great strides forward – particularly if they are able to keep a diary that records this. Clients, who at the time are mystified about how things have improved, often come to see connections at a later date when they are able to reflect on events. In the middle of a crisis it is sometimes difficult to see the wood for the trees.

Although some changes that take place are completely outside the client's control, many changes are the result of altered perceptions or modifications in the client's behaviour. When the counsellor probes for more detail around the changes, the client is often able to recall incidents that help to build a bigger picture of what is happening. Building this picture is a product of the interaction between the counsellor and the client. Indeed, McKeel and Weiner-Davis (1995) found that when counsellors asked their clients the pre-session change question in a way that implied their situations had *not* changed since they made the appointment, 67 per cent reported their situation was the same. It would seem that if the counsellor does not believe in pre-session change, then neither does the client!

When exploring the ebb and flow of change in the client's life, the counsellor paces and times the questions that form the main type of intervention employed. Questions open therapeutic space and offer the client new or different ways of thinking about situations. The counsellor is curious about solutions already in place in the client's life. As the counsellor consistently uses solution-focused, change-orientated language, clients become recruited into the vocabulary, to such an extent that they will introduce solution-focused interventions when the counsellor has gone off track. Typical questions used to create the climate of change are:

- 'What is happening in your life at the moment to make you feel hopeful that you can change the situation?'
- 'What in particular made you feel that this was a good time to come and talk things over?'
- 'What will be the benefit to you when you manage to make the change you want?'

Clients expect time and space to tell their story. They want to get things 'off their chests'. As we all know, this in itself can be therapeutic and in some cases is enough to move someone forward. Most clients would not feel safe to explore future changes without the experience of being heard, believed and respected in the present. Nylund and Corsiglia (1994) describe a misuse of SFT that pressurises clients to develop solutions before they are ready as solution-'forced' therapy. This is a mistake made by some novice solution-focused counsellors. As the counsellor pushes for solutions prematurely, the client resists and the counsellor presses the case for change even harder. This can happen when the practitioner is carrying a heavy caseload and is under time pressure to produce outcomes. One of the key skills in being an effective solution-focused practitioner is a sense of timing – to know when to back off, when to go slowly and when to move forward with the client. Learning to trust the process helps the practitioner to relax and trust the client's own sense of timing about solutions. Anxiety to produce results quickly can lead to missing the positive things the client is saying. One of the things that non-counsellor practitioners need to unlearn when they come to use the solution-focused approach is their role as problem-solvers. It takes time to learn how to resist the urge to think that your solutions are superior to anything the client comes up with. When there is silence from clients there is the temptation to intervene by 'selling' a strategy or a number of strategies to them. There is, I think, a place for this, but only as an exception rather than a rule. Effective solution-focused work requires the full repertoire of interpersonal skills needed by all counsellors:

- active listening
- empathy
- goal-setting
- immediacy
- minimal prompts
- paraphrasing
- open questioning
- reframing
- use of metaphors
- ability to handle endings.

Putting our problem into the public sphere takes courage. When a person has kept her own counsel and has spent hours mulling over the problem in her head, bringing it out into the open changes it. It can bring home the reality or non-reality of the problem. Hearing our attempts to articulate inner thoughts and feelings tests out how much we really believe them. In some cases hearing the words spoken out loud makes one realise that it is not such a big problem at all or it is different from how it sounded when it was inside one's head!

Naming a problem can relieve anxiety, guilt and bring reassurance, hope or reality to it. It can reduce the power it had over the person. Validating the reality of a problem can help society to resource its treatment, as we have seen recently with Chronic Fatigue Syndrome (ME). Going public enables self-help groups to develop and the individuals involved to know that they have not been imagining or exaggerating their situation.

Attitudes towards change are culturally conditioned. In a multicultural society there are divergent philosophies with divergent teachings about the extent to which individuals can control their destinies and how desirable it is for them to attempt to do so. As a generalisation, the Western view is that we can shape our futures actively and personally, whereas an Eastern perspective is that individuals should accept what life brings to them in a spirit of resignation. In an open society there will be degrees of synthesis between the different perspectives. This reinforces the importance of the solution-focused practitioner taking the 'one down' position and being curious about 'what works' in the cultural environment of the client.

In the first session the immediate task of the solution-focused counsellor is to validate and acknowledge the client's feelings and concerns. These concerns will not only involve the problem but also any possible solution. Many people will fear that making changes is beyond their ability or that change may even make the situation worse in some way. Others may fear that once a change process starts there is no way of controlling where it will end. Some may prefer to stay with 'the devil you know.' People swing between problem-talk and solution-talk. I find it helpful to think of this movement in terms of two islands – problem island and solution island (O'Connell, 2001). When the client first comes for help she is on problem island. This is territory with which she is very familiar. She knows every tiny piece of the island – for most of her life it has been the only place she has known, as she can't remember times she has spent off the island. Perhaps everyone else she knows is also on problem island. If the helper gains the trust of the client, he will be allowed to visit the client's problem island and if he sounds genuinely interested, the client will give him a tour of the island and tell him about events linked with different parts of it. The client will have a lot of stories to tell about life on problem island. When he has completed the tour of the island with the client, the counsellor needs to do something different, otherwise they will both be stuck on problem island, possibly going round it endlessly. There is no point in the counsellor going off to solution island on his own, leaving the client on problem island. So, by asking solution-orientated questions, he invites the client to think about leaving problem island for a while and exploring what solution-focused island would be like and how and when she would get there (Bramwell, 2003). If the client succeeds in doing this, it may only be for a short while until the security of the problem island comfort zone calls her back. Hopefully she will continue to make visits to solution island until she feels able to spend longer periods there. At some stage the client might even live on the edge of problem island nearest to solution island or designate a solution spot on problem island (Melchior, 2003). If her experience of visiting solution island was positive, she will know where to go when she needs to escape problem island for a while. She may even become a solution island resident, although, given that life is full of good and bad times, she might sometimes travel back to problem island.

For some clients, making the move to solution-talk is just not possible at that moment. There is too big a gap between their negative feelings and engaging in conversation about a better future or how their present situation contains positives as well as negatives. In such a case the counsellor needs to allow the client as much time as she needs to engage in problem-talk. Their conversation may focus more on coping strategies and what helps to stop the situation deteriorating than on what could be done to help it improve. Containing the problem or damage limitation may be the only strategy available. It is very difficult to stop some clients from talking at great length about their problems. A colleague agreed with her client that they would use a timer to regulate the amount of problem-talk. They agreed that when the timer went off after 15 minutes of problem-talk, they would engage in solution-talk. After a few times the client became socialised into the habit and did not need the timer. She later said that she preferred this allocation of time as she often felt worse when they focused on the problems for too long (Keen, 2003).

For some clients, focusing on and talking about the future is actually a lot easier than talking about the past. The past is a scene of conflict with many well-defended versions of history, but the future is an unwritten page. Although we all learn from our past and never really leave it behind, it can be liberating to experience a sense of new possibilities. It is significant how the atmosphere and amount of energy in an interview can change when there is a move from problem- to solution-talk.

The counsellor models the use of descriptive language to explore the client's life. She uses the client's own words to clarify the observable changes necessary to reach the client's goals. She avoids abstract and vague terms, such as depression, low self-esteem, attention-seeking behaviour and stress, in favour of concrete descriptions of the client's day-to-day behaviour. The counsellor will translate the client's conversation about feelings or attitudes or personality characteristics into examples of observable external behaviour. This emphasis on external behaviour does not, however, exclude conversation about 'inner' feelings and attitudes:

> *Counsellor:* So what are the signs for you that you're feeling depressed?
> *Client:* I stay in bed most of the day. I don't care about how I look. I hardly ever go out unless I absolutely have to. The others at home have to look after themselves, I can't even be bothered eating.
> *Counsellor:* What else is happening when you feel depressed?
> *Client:* I avoid people as much as possible. I have no energy or enthusiasm for anything. I give up doing the things I like. I feel like I want to be left on my own.

This client used the term depression to describe her experiences. Her clear pictorial language enables the counsellor to understand her unique experience of depression. From this beginning they may negotiate her goals. These might include:

- being able to get out of bed earlier
- taking more care of her appearance
- being able to go out of the house
- having more energy.

Another starting point can be a discussion about what clients know definitely does *not* work for them – their failed solutions.

Failed solutions

Identifying patterns of failed solutions is the characteristic of the Mental Research Institute (MRI) model of brief problem-focused counselling. Most solution-focused counsellors include elements of this perspective in their repertoire. The MRI model suggests that, in order to achieve a different outcome, the client needs to do something different from what she is currently doing: 'If you always do what you've always done, you'll always get what you've got.' She needs to abandon 'solutions' that have failed repeatedly in the past. This runs counter to the cultural message of, 'If at first you don't succeed, try, try and try again.' However one may choose to follow the 'philosopher' Homer Simpson who once said, 'If at first you don't succeed, it's too difficult', or even more fatalistically, 'If at first you don't succeed, then maybe failure's your thing.'

At the end of a successful course of counselling, a solution-focused counsellor might ask the client what advice she would pass on to clients with similar problems. The counsellor can dip into this fund of hard-earned wisdom by keeping good case notes or a file of therapeutic tips for clients.

Clarifying the client's goals

While we pursue the unattainable, we make impossible the realisable.

Robert Ardrey (1970)

What we call the beginning is often the end, and to make an end is to make a beginning. The end is where we start from.

T. S. Eliot, *The Four Quartets* (1963)

The counsellor helps the client define his problem in a solvable way and generate clear, simple, attainable goals. The client's goals may not always be compatible with the goals of the referrer and that can be a challenge for the counsellor. In Macdonald's (1994) study of SFT there was a significant correlation between a positive outcome and the successful negotiation of specific goals for treatment. The outcome was less successful when goals were defined negatively and least successful when the goals were non-specific. In SFT the counsellor attempts to clarify with clients what they hope will be happening should counselling be successful. This is not always possible, as clients may be vague and puzzled about their problems and equally unclear as to what would constitute a good outcome. In order to avoid drift and lack of focus, the counsellor tries to negotiate with the client a clear ending:

* What are your hopes in coming here?
* If coming here turns out to be a really good idea what differences will you notice in your life?
* What will be the first signs that things are improving?

Sometimes it can be helpful to find out how much clients feel can be achieved in a given time frame by asking them a time-projected question:

* If we were to meet in three/six months' time and you were to tell me that things were much better, what examples might you give me about helpful things you or others have done? What would have been the first thing that happened?

The counsellor listens carefully to all that the client says and builds closely on each response. He is listening for evidence of what works for this client and what will facilitate change. For some clients, their 'solution' is that there is no external solution. Coming to terms with the fact that there is no clear resolution to a problem requires strengths, qualities and strategies.

It also helps when people appreciate that their feelings may not change at the same time as they change their behaviour. Similarly, clients do not need to feel positive before they act to improve their situation. It is more likely that they will feel better when they act constructively.

The solution-focused practitioner will be guided by what works for the client, often thinking in terms of incremental changes – small steps forward that extend the constructive work the client is already doing. These steps often emerge from exploring the exceptions to the problem and answers to the miracle question.

The miracle question

> You must give birth to your images. They are the future waiting to be born ... fear not the strangeness you feel. The future must enter into you long before it happens.
>
> Rainer Maria Rilke (1990: 115)

The miracle question is the intervention most associated with the solution-focused school. In my experience it is much misunderstood and misused by those with only a casual acquaintance with the model. It is typically used in a first session, but also in subsequent sessions. It aims to elicit evidence from the client of existing solutions and resources and to clarify goals. It is a future-orientated question that helps the client describe, as clearly and specifically as possible, what her life will be like once she solves the problem or manages it better.

There are variations to it, but the standard formula, as devised by Steve de Shazer (1988), is:

> Imagine when you go to sleep one night a miracle happens and the problems we've been talking about disappear. As you were asleep, you didn't know that a miracle had happened. When you woke up, what would be the first signs for you that a miracle had happened?

This question is similar to Adler's 'fundamental question' – 'What would be different if all your problems were solved?' (1925). It is also similar to Erickson's crystal ball technique, in which he invited clients to look into the future and then explain how what had happened had come about. He also used the technique of inviting clients to imagine a date on a calendar when things were better, then to work backwards to see what had happened at various points along the way.

In using the miracle question it is helpful to introduce it slowly and reflectively, with pauses between the phrases to allow the client to enter into the spirit of the question. It is an exercise in the imagination, but not a fantasy journey. It enables clients to rise above negative, problem-dominated thinking and articulate their preferred future. Not all clients find this easy to do. Many feel stuck in the past with no belief that their future will be any different or better. It is a fact that many people have limited choices and little power to shape their lives. In many contexts and environments it is the organisation or society that needs the miracle, not the individual. However, whatever our circumstances, our level of happiness or peace can be assisted by re-evaluating our responses.

The miracle question can help the client to clarify goals and the means to achieve them. It can identify existing solutions and resources while creating a climate of change. Though it raises the possibility of life being different, it should not generate false hopes, which cause disillusionment or even despair. The questioner does not hype up the client's responses. The intention is to generate a rich, detailed, practical description of life without the problem. Being able to visualise the future can be empowering and instructive in teaching us how to act in the present.

EXAMPLE

Counsellor: Let me ask you an unusual question, Anne, that many people find helpful.

This introduction forewarns the client that the next question is surprising, but suggests that trying to answer it will be worth the effort because other people have gained from it.

Counsellor: Imagine that when you go to sleep tonight a miracle happens and all of the difficulties that you have been having at home disappear. Because you are asleep, you don't know that a miracle has happened. When you wake up in the morning, what will be the first signs for you that a miracle has happened?

Client: I don't know. *[Pause]*

This is a frequent initial response. It is important that the practitioner is not thrown by it. Here are some responses that can help:

- Being silent and giving the client the chance to think about it.
- Telling the client that there is no right or wrong answer.
- Asking the client again, 'What do you think?'
- Asking, 'What do you think that you might notice was better?'
- Asking, 'What would anyone else notice about you when the miracle happened?'

Sometimes clients answer in fantasy mode, saying 'I'll be rich, have a big house, the perfect partner …' These replies can evoke lighthearted banter, yet still reveal some serious hopes. At the opposite end of the spectrum I have met clients whose initial answer to the miracle question was, 'I'll be dead.' This requires a discussion about how and why this feels like a solution for the client. Having acknowledged this (and made some form of risk assessment), the counsellor invites the client to describe another version of the morning after the miracle, in which their problems were being dealt with, but the client was still alive. On some occasions the miracle question can be cathartic, with clients bursting into tears and disclosing a trauma that would end if a miracle happened. It would be a mistake for the counsellor to always expect a positive answer to the question.

Returning to our client above. After supportive prompting she might say:

Client: Maybe we'd feel closer together.
Counsellor: How do you picture you both feeling closer to each other?
Client: We'd feel relaxed and calm and just generally happier.

While validating the client's feelings, it is also helpful to translate them into observable behaviour. Fisch (1994) offers a variation of the miracle question:

> Assume you wake up tomorrow morning and, for some reason or another, the feeling you have is no longer a problem, what will be different then? How will you know?

As Quick (1994) points out, this creates two possible scenarios: one in which the feeling has gone and a second where the feeling is still there but is somehow no longer a problem.

If a client states what will *not* be happening once the miracle happens – for example, he won't be worried any longer – the counsellor needs to ask him what he will be doing *instead* of worrying.

Counsellor: So what would you be doing differently if you were feeling more relaxed and happy now that the miracle has happened?
Client: I'd be getting on with my partner.
Counsellor: So how would the day start and how would you notice things were different?
Client: We'd get up together and, if it wasn't a work day, we'd spend some time planning what we were going to do together.
Counsellor: So what else would be happening?

The phrase 'what else?' is a recurring one in SFT as practitioners use it to obtain detailed answers to questions such as scaling, the miracle question and exception seeking. When you can't think what else to say, say 'what else'!

Clients may want to explore more than one answer to the miracle question – for example, what the miracle would look like if they stayed in the relationship or what it would look like if they ended it. Counsellors unfamiliar with solution-focused methods sometimes have difficulty in exploring the answer to the miracle question in sufficient detail. It takes time to develop the questioning needed to keep clients on the 'solution track.' It is important to develop these skills as the specific and graphic qualities of the answer are crucial for the success of the process.

Client: He'd be able to take criticism without getting angry.
Counsellor: Would you be giving it differently because you were feeling more relaxed and happy?

The miracle question aims to reveal how the client could act to improve the situation. In this exchange the counsellor suggests that the client may need to act differently to help bring about a more peaceful relationship.

Client: Probably, yes, a little bit more subtly.
Counsellor: *What would that mean for you?*
Client: I'd do it without shouting at him.
Counsellor: How would he respond to that?
Client: Better, because that's the only way things are going to be solved, by talking about things.

The counsellor explores the unique strategies this client would adopt to change the communication pattern between her and her partner. The client has already suggested that she knows what to do, but it is usually helpful to encourage her to be specific and describe exactly what she would do. The counsellor occupies a 'one down' (non-expert) position, curious to know what the client has in mind. His prompting is offered in a tentative way, allowing the client to put forward her own version.

Counsellor: So, if things were a lot better, you'd both be sitting down and you'd be able to communicate more clearly without upsetting each other and be able to say what it is you'd like to happen, what you would like him to do, what he would like you to do. So what would you be talking about?
Client: Probably about me having some more help with the kids. If I ask him to do anything he just says he's too busy, but he comes round later if I leave him alone.

In the client's final sentence we see a combination of problem-talk ('he just says he's too busy') and solution-talk ('but he comes round later if I leave him alone'). This problem–solution polarity often figures in the responses. At this point the counsellor listens and empathises, but does not expand the problem-talk as this slows down the client's momentum towards solutions. If a client is allowing problem-talk to sabotage the miracle answer, the counsellor reminds her that in this conversation the miracle has actually happened, so the problem has been overcome.

Counsellor: So, if you were handling it just the way you'd like, you'd be able to ask about getting help without him feeling. ...
Client: That I'm getting at him.
Counsellor: How do you do it at the moment? What would need to happen for you to do that again?

The counsellor and the client, having identified a desired change in behaviour, now negotiate which strategies may help to bring about the change.

There is a specific interest in currently successful strategies that the client could develop further. In the first instance the counsellor tries to find out whether or not any existing strategies are working. If they are, the client might consider how to maintain or even extend them; if they are not, he may be willing to discard them and do something different. When clients feel that nothing is working and they have tried everything, the counsellor needs to be supportive and empathic and not pressurise the client into being more optimistic. Believing that the client is cooperating as well as he can, the counsellor will not force the pace but move at the client's tempo.

Clients often become animated and energetic when answering the miracle question. The atmosphere in the room often changes and both client and counsellor become more energised. Publicly expressing their hopes in the miracle answer can in itself help to motivate people towards their goals. Clients often report how surprised they were by their answers to the miracle question.

The counsellor helps the client to develop answers to the miracle question by active listening, prompting, empathising and therapeutic questioning. She does this in the following way.

- By inviting the client to describe in detail the day after the miracle and exploring how the differences in one part of the day will affect the other.

  Counsellor: So when things go much better at work, what will it be like when you come home in the evening?

  Counsellor: When you manage to handle the children better during the day, what will be happening in the evening?

- By using circular questions about other significant people and how the miracle would affect them.

  - Who will be the first person to notice a miracle has happened? How will they react?
  - What difference will that make to you?
  - How will you know that they have found out?
  - How will your partner/friend behave now that the miracle has happened?

Questions may focus on feelings as well as behaviour.

- How will you feel if you manage to do that?

Is it always appropriate to use the miracle question? Some practitioners advocate caution when using it in sensitive situations – for example, when the client has a terminal illness or has suffered a recent bereavement. These are situations when the anticipated answer to the miracle question is something unattainable, such as a bereaved person wanting the return of the person who has died. Some counsellors customise the miracle question in order to pre-empt a potentially distressing answer. Others prefer to 'work with what you've got' and argue that much helpful information can come from the question, even in these circumstances (Butler and Powers, 1996). In my experience it is impossible to predict how particular clients will react to the question. When I have felt most hesitant about asking it, I have often had the most productive responses and vice versa.

Sometimes a modified form of the miracle question feels more appropriate. Here are some possible alternative versions.

- If you were aiming to bring about change in this area of your life, what will be the first signs that you were making progress?
- If you went in to work (or school, home or wherever the problem takes place) tomorrow and all your problems were solved, what would have happened?
- Suppose you were starting (your job, this relationship or whatever) again, what would you like to be different?
- If you came to work (home, school) tomorrow and the situation that was causing you distress had been removed, what do you think you would notice?

The miracle question is a powerful tool in groupwork and in couple and family counselling. Each member offers his or her own version of life without the problem. This can be an enlightening experience for other family members. A variation is to use circular questioning to enable one client to predict how the other will answer the miracle question. The ensuing discussion can help to move on people who have been stuck in blaming, negative and critical frames of mind. In conflict situations the counsellor tries to highlight the common ground, encourages clients to listen to each other's requests and modify unreasonable demands. In particular, the counsellor compliments them on what they are doing already to solve the problem. One way in which to move on from the miracle question is to introduce scaling for one or more parts of the miracle.

Scaling in a first session

In a digital age, when words fail, numbers can come to our rescue. Given the complexity of human relationships, we frequently fail to grasp the meaning of other peoples' communications with us. We blithely assume we know what they are talking about, but often this assumption proves unfounded. De Shazer and his colleagues (de Shazer and Berg, 1992) began to use scaling in their work as they found that clients could use it to express what they meant, even when the meaning was not clear to anyone else. The client's self-understanding was more important than the counsellor's understanding of the client.

```
10  ↑  Best it could be
 9
 8
 7
 6
 5
 4
 3
 2
 1
 0  │  Worst it has been
```

Figure 4.1 *Scaling*

The counsellor uses a scale of zero to ten (see Figure 4.1), with ten representing the best it could be and zero representing rock bottom, the worst it has been (or perhaps how the client felt before contacting the service). The primary purpose of scaling questions is to help clients set small identifiable goals, measure progress (beginning, middle and end) and establish priorities for action. They can also be used to assess client motivation and confidence; in fact, they can be used with virtually any aspect of the counselling process. Scaling questions do not follow any specific sequence but the examples below are illustrations:

- On a scale of zero to ten, with ten representing the best it can be and zero the worst, where would you say you are today?
- Where would you say you were a day or two ago?
- What was happening at the time when you were higher?
- If you've gone down, how did you stop yourself going further down?
- In the past, have you ever been higher up the scale? How did that happen?
- Where would you realistically hope to get to in the next few days/ weeks?
- Would staying where you are on the scale be good enough for now, given all the pressures on you?
- If you move up the scale, what will be happening that will tell you that you have arrived at that point?
- What would need to happen for you to move up one point on the scale in the next few days?
- What do you know you need to do, or not do, to prevent you from going down the scale?
- What might sabotage your efforts and how could you resist?
- What do you know about yourself that makes you hopeful that you can achieve what you want in this situation?
- What have you learned from other times in your life that would be useful to you now?
- What skill/quality/strength would be really helpful for you at the moment?

It is likely that the counsellor will use scaling questions in the first sessions and throughout subsequent sessions. It is a practical tool that clients can use between sessions. The use of numbers is purely arbitrary, but it is client defined. There is no attempt by the counsellor to challenge where the client puts herself on the scale, even if the evidence for that judgement seems unclear or doubtful to the counsellor.

The following is an excerpt from a first interview in which the client reports that she and her partner have separated and are considering divorce.

EXAMPLE

Client: He says that he wants me to go back to him.
Counsellor: On a scale of zero to ten, ten being you are absolutely sure you want to go back and zero being it's absolutely out of the question, where do you feel you are at the moment?
Client: About six and that's being generous considering how he's treated me. If you had asked me last week I would have said one.

The client is making three points here:

• my sense of trust is in a state of flux and could go up or down
• I have managed to change my attitude or behaviour, despite feeling low
• I have changed in the direction of us getting back together again.

This change has not been without cost and she might need a period in which she consolidates her six or reconsiders her position.

Counsellor: How did you get from one to six?
Client: It's helped just getting away from him for a few days. I asked him to stop pestering me with phone calls and letters and he has. I've also been remembering how hard a time he's been through as well, losing his job. Maybe we both need help. He never talks to anyone.

The client demonstrates her commitment to tackling the problem. She is taking time to think through the problem as well as trying to see things from his point of view.

Counsellor: How did you manage to do that? It was a big jump for you getting to six wasn't it?
Client: I think perhaps because I know that this might be our last chance. We can't carry on the way we were – it's got to change one way or another. If we can agree on a few things I would be willing to give it a last try.
Counsellor: What do you think you are doing differently because it feels like a last chance this time?

Client:	I've stopped criticising him in front of the children. When he's asked to see them, I haven't made it difficult. If we're going to get back together, he's got to get on better with the kids.
Counsellor:	Where do you think he is on the scale in terms of wanting to come back?
Client:	About the same. I think we're both a little bit unsure of one another at the moment.

Scales can be useful in working with not only the perceptions of the identified client but also with those of partners, friends or colleagues.

Counsellor:	You're both at six now. Is that good enough for you to start living together again or do you need to get to seven or what?
Client:	I think we need to be six for longer before he should come back.
Counsellor:	What would need to happen to keep you both at six for the next week or two?
Client:	He needs to show me he's serious about giving me the support I need.
Counsellor:	What would be the first signs for you that he was getting better at that?
Client:	He would listen to me when I tell him what I'm feeling and not be so selfish in the way he always puts himself first. He thinks it's all right for him to go on about his problems, but as soon as I start telling him how hard it's been at home with the kids, he doesn't want to know.
Counsellor:	So you'll feel more confident about being a six when he starts to listen to you more than he does at the moment. Anything else?
Client:	He'll let me know where he is and not come home at all hours of the night.
Counsellor:	What difference would that make for you?
Client:	I'd trust him more. At the moment 1 don't know what he's up to.

The discussion about how to keep at six elicits a description of the observable behaviour that the client wants from her partner. When the client expresses what she wants in negative terms (what will *not* be happening), the counsellor rephrases it in positive terms (what *will* be happening instead).

Assessing motivation

A dream without a vision is a daydream, a vision without a dream is a nightmare.

Origins unknown

We tend to work towards goals of our own choosing. When others set goals for us we might comply under duress or politeness, but we often find ways to sabotage them. One of the strengths of solution-focused work is the way in which it stays very close to the client's own goals and does not try to convert them to something else.

EXAMPLE

Counsellor:	On a scale of zero to ten, ten being you would do anything to overcome these panic attacks and zero being you would really love to but you don't think you will do anything, where would you put yourself today?
Client:	Three.
Counsellor:	Will three be good enough to make a start?
Client:	No. I feel I've tried everything and nothing works. I've almost given up hope that it could get any better.
Counsellor:	So although you've had a lot of setbacks you've managed to keep trying? Some people would have completely given up. How have you kept going?
Client:	We've always been fighters in my family. My mum taught me to keep at it when things weren't going well.
Counsellor:	So if she was here she would say keep fighting?
Client:	Yes.
Counsellor:	Where would you need to get to on the scale before you felt you had a chance of fighting off the panic attacks?
Client:	Five.
Counsellor:	How will you know when you've got to five?
Client:	If I could relax more. I feel so tense most of the time, it keeps giving me headaches and then I feel like giving up.
Counsellor:	How would you go about being relaxed enough to feel you were getting to five?
Client:	I don't know.
Counsellor:	When the sun comes out for you and you feel less tense than usual what has helped to make you better?
Client:	When I'm on my own and I can listen to my own music.
Counsellor:	Anything else?
Client:	I like Fridays when I don't have to go to work. I can lie in and potter around a bit.
Counsellor:	Does that mean that if this Friday you put on your music and had an easy start to the day, you'd possibly feel a five and more able to fight back against the panic attacks?
Client:	I think so.
Counsellor:	If you're a three today, what would help to get you to be a four?

Similar questions may explore the client's level of confidence in relation to the problem.

Discovering the client's resources

Competence seeking
The counsellor sets out to discover and affirm the resources, strengths and qualities that the client can utilise to 'solve' the problem (de Shazer, 1988).

It is not enough to identify resources, it is necessary to understand how they were deployed and how to reactivate them. The current problem situation may differ from previous ones in which the client coped, but there is often an identifiable pattern – for example, the client's previous experience of loss. A client who felt suicidal after the death of her mother experienced similar thoughts and feelings on the breakdown of her marriage. With the counsellor, she recalled how she had coped with her grief and considered how she might use those resources again.

We know that many people with psychological problems are 'spontaneous improvers' and that most people do not seek professional help when they experience problems in life. Such people adapt to the problems that their environment creates by using skills, beliefs, character qualities and social networks as and when needed. In solution-focused work, we seek to bring those resources into the awareness of the client. This does not mean that clients possess fully formed solutions within themselves, but they have the potential to solve their own problems. They may need a counsellor to help them own and apply their resources or extend or modify their existing repertoire of life skills.

Exception seeking
In this intervention, the counsellor engages the client in seeking exceptions to the problem – that is, those times when the problem was not present or was being managed better. Chevalier (1995), borrowing from de Shazer, makes a useful distinction between deliberate and spontaneous exceptions.

Deliberate exceptions take place when people do something that they can see made a difference to the problem and they feel capable of repeating. What they did or stopped doing altered the problem situation for the better and would be worth trying again. This need not mean that the client repeat exactly what worked last time there was an exception. The circumstances may have changed so that mere repetition is no longer appropriate. Mechanically repeating actions may even be part of the problem!

EXAMPLE

Jim was very clear that he needed a range of techniques to use when he had panic attacks. He knew that nothing worked for very long for him. He developed a hierarchy of strategies to use depending on the severity of the attack. For him it was important to know that he had mental strategies (recite the alphabet backwards, for example), as well as physical (relaxed breathing), psychological (self-talk) and visual (picturing himself as strong and coping) ones, that he could vary to meet the challenge facing him at the time.

Spontaneous exceptions are those occasions when, for some mysterious reason or for some reason beyond the person's control, the problem did not happen or was not as bad as it usually is. The client does not feel that this had anything to do with her or believes that it was due to certain circumstances that are unlikely to be repeated. As far as the client is concerned, they were welcome surprises but these incidents have nothing to contribute to solving the problem. Exceptions are more useful when the client sees them as relevant and significant.

With deliberate exceptions the counsellor will encourage the client to keep doing what worked and even expand on it if possible. With spontaneous exceptions, the client will be invited to notice when they happen and observe whether or not they had any degree of control over them. Even when it is not possible to work out how they happened, they can still be celebrated. They can still teach us something if we look hard enough.

EXAMPLE

Client: I've not been so stressed the past week.
Counsellor: How did you manage that?
Client: I was on holiday.
Counsellor: How did you manage to relax on your holiday?
Client: It was great being out of the hostile atmosphere. After a couple of days I really unwound and managed to forget about it. It's going to be hard going back.
Counsellor: How did you succeed in forgetting about work for a bit? That must have been difficult?
Client: It took me a while, but I was determined that it was not going to ruin my holiday. I didn't leave a phone number so I couldn't be contacted and I told my partner to stop me if I started to talk shop.
Counsellor: So when you were able to switch off that helped. Do you ever manage to do that when you're at home?
Client: No, I feel work takes over my life.
Counsellor: As well as switching off, what else did you do that helped on holiday?
Client: Having some peace and quiet was wonderful. Not having people wanting something from me all the time. Having time for myself.
Counsellor: What did you enjoy most when you had time to yourself?
Client: I enjoyed doing nothing. I read some novels, which I haven't done for ages, and listened to some of my music.
Counsellor: So you know that finding time to be on your own, somewhere relatively peaceful and quiet where you can just crash or read or listen to music, really helps you to cope with stress.
Client: Yes. I wish I could take a long, long holiday!
Counsellor: Even if that were not possible, is there anything you did or did not do on holiday that you would like to keep doing or not doing and, if so, how could you ensure that it happens?

The exploration of the circumstances ('Where?', 'What?', 'When?', 'How?') around exceptions will cover not only what the client actually did but also how she was thinking at the time – what self-talk she used and how she felt before, during and after the exception. How other significant people reacted to the exception–can also be revealing. The counsellor might ask, 'What difference did it make to your colleagues/friend/partner/children when this exception took place?' The counsellor may also challenge the client to become more aware of how her use of language either increases or decreases the number of exceptions. Clients can begin to realise that when they say, 'I always fail/get angry/feel stupid and so on', they actually mean, 'Sometimes I fail/get angry/feel stupid so that means sometimes I don't.' We see what we choose to pay attention to and we often get more of what we talk about. As Anaïs Ninn once said, 'we do not see things as they are, but as we are.' We need to use filters that capture more of the positives and let more of the negatives through. Blaming, critical, destructive talk only sets up a cycle of frustration, guilt and failure. If we only notice the mistakes, the failures, the shortcomings, we will be missing vital evidence. We can and do learn from mistakes and failures of course, but we can also get trapped in a vicious circle of over-analysis of times when things went wrong at the expense of learning from times when things went right.

Exceptions provide a glimpse of a possible future and provide clues for tracking solutions, as well as evidence for discarding failed strategies. For clients used to professionals concentrating exclusively on their problems, this experience of solution seeking can come as a refreshing change. Highlighting evidence of non-problem behaviour affirms clients' competence and resources, increases their confidence and motivation and raises their level of optimism and hope. Quick (1994) makes the point that even when clients are unclear as to how they made an exception happen, the attention to the event sows the seeds of solutions. Awareness of exceptions can also raise awareness of significant values, such as a client who regularly drinks and drives but never does it when her grandchildren are in the car. Keying into these values may create enough motivation for other changes. The interviewer can also use evidence of a recent exception to invite the client to reflect on its distant history – 'I bet that didn't come out of the blue, did it? Have you done something like that before at some time? Did someone encourage you to do that?' and so on.

White (1989) describes exceptions as 'unique outcomes' that tell alternative stories about the client. Clients often have strongly developed problem-focused narratives, but underdeveloped solution narratives. By encouraging an over-elaboration of the problem-focused narrative, the client can come to feel less and less able to change his 'problem identity' by himself and more dependent on the counsellor to do it for him. In SFT, the counsellor facilitates the generation of alternative solution stories that orientate the person towards a new empowering identity. Exceptions are a gateway to a new life story. Eliciting exceptions does not, however, always produce immediate results. If, when you are learning to drive, you stall the car each time you try to start it, you tend to dismiss the one time you moved off smoothly as an inexplicable aberration, beginner's luck! As the frequency of the exceptions increases and becomes the rule, attention moves to the next problem area – reversing round corners! After a while, you forget you ever had a problem with starting. The more we can help clients to expand their awareness of exceptions, the more they reduce the influence of the problem.

In my experience, if you ask a client directly, 'Have there been times recently when you have not had the problem or it has been in some way better?', most will instinctively respond in the negative. Later in the interview they may unwittingly provide evidence of exceptions. I tend to listen between the lines for evidence of exceptions then find a supportive way of exploring these with the client. I will listen for phrases such as:

- 'Most of the time'
- 'Normally'
- 'At the moment'
- 'It's up and down'

- 'Quite often'
- 'Sometimes'
- 'So far'
- 'It's not so bad'

These suggest either that there have been exceptions in the past or that the client has not given up hope about exceptions in the future.

Exploring tasks

'The message'
SFT clients will know from pre-counselling information that, towards the end of each session, the counsellor will take a short break in order to compose the feedback – or 'the message', as it is known in SFT. Before taking the break, the counsellor checks that the client has nothing further to add. Some practitioners actually leave the room to think about what to give as feedback to the client; others take a few moments while remaining in the room with the client. Sometimes it is possible to hand over the end process to the client, so that she summarises her achievements and indicates what her next step will be.

The feedback follows a standard structure, as shown in Figure 4.2.

Give client positive feedback.
Summarise client's achievements.
Link to client's goals.
Negotiate a task.

Figure 4.2

GIVE CLIENT POSITIVE FEEDBACK
Typically, the first part of 'the message' consists of giving positive feedback to the client about his constructive contributions in the session – such as his courage in coming and the honesty of his contribution.

The feedback should be:

- based on the evidence of what happened in the actual interview
- short, clearly marking the conclusion of the session
- fine-tuned in line with the way it is being received by the client
- credibly positive without being far fetched or overly optimistic
- genuine, with the counsellor only saying what she believes.

The feedback may include phrases such as:

- 'I'd like to say how much I have appreciated... .'
- 'I was impressed with... .'
- 'I thought it was great that you... .'

This ensures that the client receives credit for the efforts she has already made to overcome personal and environmental difficulties. The giving of non-patronising compliments, helps to reduce the power gap between the client and the counsellor and can increase the sense of collaboration. Genuine compliments – as distinct from manipulative flattery – help to motivate people, especially those with long experience of failure and isolation. A client once said to me that when someone pays her a compliment, she always waits for a 'but' that will undermine the positive. When no 'but' appeared in the feedback from the counsellor she was able to welcome the feedback unconditionally. The positivity of the feedback needs to be tailored to the needs of the individual client and take into account pertinent gender and cultural issues.

SUMMARISE CLIENT'S ACHIEVEMENTS

In the next step, the counsellor summarises positive strategies that the client has already begun to use. She will encourage the client to consolidate what is already proving to be helpful. The following is an excerpt from a message delivered to a client who had been suffering from stress.

EXAMPLE

Counsellor: What has really impressed me today has been you knowing your own mind. ... You've developed a degree of self-awareness that is proving helpful to you. ... You're translating that awareness into behaviour so that, as you become aware of a situation, ... you're telling yourself 'I don't have to follow the old script. I can do this differently. I don't have to go from 0 to 60 in 5 seconds'. ... You've developed techniques for preventing problems from building up ... like the way you register automatic thoughts but don't let them overpower you. ... I think you're really trying to move down a gear and, usually when you move down a gear, you get more control of the car. You've taught yourself to slow down.

LINK TO CLIENT'S GOALS

If possible, the counsellor will make a bridging statement that links the client's resources and achievements to the goals of the client.

> *Counsellor*: The way you managed to walk away on Thursday when they were winding you up sounded like the sort of thing that would be helpful when you get frustrated and fed up with your manager at work.

NEGOTIATE A TASK

In the early days of solution-focused practice, under the influence of strategic counselling, giving clients tasks to perform (homework) was an essential part of the process. These tasks were often devised by the practitioner and clients were expected to comply. This emphasis has now largely disappeared from practice. Nowadays, the counsellor simply encourages the client to 'keep doing what works.' This should not be difficult because an effective interview will have elicited evidence of what works, as well as the client's strengths, resources and hopes for the future. In addition to this type of task, the counsellor may suggest:

- notice tasks
- randomised tasks
- do something different tasks
- pretend tasks.

NOTICE TASKS   Notice tasks might be suggested to clients who have:

- struggled to identify exceptions to the problem
- are unclear in their answers to the miracle question
- have few ideas about what they could do to make things better.

This non-threatening task invites the client to observe:

- times when something constructive or positive happens
- times when someone else does something that they find helpful
- times when the expected problem fails to appear or is managed better
- parts of their lives that they would like to see continue.

One form of the notice task known as the 'formula first session task' (FFST) (de Shazer and Molnar, 1984: 297) was originally used at the end of the first session:

> Until the next time we meet, I'd like you just to observe what things are happening in your life/family/work that you'd like to see continue then come back and tell me about it.

RANDOMISED TASKS   When a client feels torn between conflicting options, the counsellor invites her to make a choice on a purely arbitrary basis by, for example, tossing a coin or changing strategies on alternative days. Clients can then decide on the basis of their experience of trying them in practice.

DO SOMETHING DIFFERENT TASKS   'Do something different' is something of a solution-focused axiom based on the premise that 'if you always do what you've always done, you'll always get what you've got' (in fact you'll probably end up losing that as well!) What the 'something different' should be is a decision for the client to make. It is an invitation to experiment and break out of the old, problem-focused routine and perhaps find something much better.

PRETEND TASKS   Hawkes et al. (1998) report the usefulness of this task. A pretend task is one in which the client is invited to act 'as if the miracle has already happened.' In the video, 'The Right Path or the Other Path?' (de Shazer, 1998), de Shazer invites his young client to imagine for one hour each morning that the miracle has happened. For her, the miracle was that she was getting on better with her parents, off drugs, going to school more often, getting her life together. When she pretended this for one hour, she found that her parents reacted in very supportive and affirming ways and she ended up 'acting out' her miracle for much longer than one hour each day. Her imaginative strategy became a breakthrough to a better life.

WHICH TASK?
First sessions may include some or all of the above interventions. Obviously the exact blend and balance will change with each client. Being solution-focused is a creative enterprise in which client and counsellor 'live in the moment'. This is not counselling by numbers so there can be no set template for each session. The counsellor is committed to cooperating with the clients in ways that work for them, suiting their personalities and values.

Practice points

- If you don't listen to your clients, they won't listen to you.
- Always give the client credit.
- Go slowly at the beginning of the work.
- Ask yourself whether or not you keep the client on 'problem island.'
- You don't have to start with history-taking, you can start with future-talk.
- Search for exceptions.

5

Second Sessions and Beyond: Keeping the Focus on Solutions

If not you, who? If not now, when?

Rabbi Hillel, cited in Hoyt (1995)

What makes this a problem? Why now?

Slive, MacLaurin, Oakander and Amundson (1995)

In describing second and subsequent sessions, I feel compelled to issue the same therapeutic health warning given at the start of the last chapter. Textbook clients do not exist and practitioners are not automatons. Each client has a unique combination of needs and abilities, so, for some, change can be sudden and dramatic, while for others it is slow and difficult. The outline of a second session is therefore only a guide, not a definitive script. The model serves the client, not the client the model. There is no mechanical formula. O'Hanlon and Weiner-Davis (1989: 77) graphically describe the therapeutic process as:

> a bit like rock climbing. You have an idea of the goal, but the actual scaling of the mountain involves using general methods of rock climbing adapted to a particular mountain. Sometimes you may even have to break the rule of the accepted method to reach the goal. The mountain will 'teach' you how to scale it. Likewise, clients have taught us how to help them reach their goals and sometimes they have taught us that it will take something other than our usual procedures to get there.

Aims of the second session

In cooperation with the client, the aims of second and subsequent sessions are to:

- consolidate constructive change
- review task performance, where appropriate
- construct solutions
- develop new strategies for change
- continue to deconstruct the problem
- evaluate and plan the ending.

These do not follow a prescribed sequence. Some solution-focused practitioners start the second session by asking, 'What's changed, what's better or what's different?' Others adopt a less direct approach and accept that the client is likely to want to report on the past week, with its successes and its failures. If the client needs to engage in further discussion of the problem, it is important to listen with respect and attentiveness. The client may need to retell stories or provide new ones until he feels sure that the counsellor understands and is trustworthy. As she listens, she is able to hear how the client constructs his world. At the same time, the conversation enables the client to 'reality test' current and potential courses of action. In addition to listening to the client, the counsellor can ask coping and scaling questions from the very start, as long as it does not feel to the client that the problem is being trivialised or that the counsellor is being oppressively optimistic.

Consolidating constructive change

'The purpose of each successive session is to assess change and to help to maintain it so that a solution can be achieved' (Lipchik and de Shazer, 1986). This focus on change must be achieved in a climate that allows the client to feel safe and respected. As the counsellor asks questions, the focus moves from the general to the particular in relation to the client's perspective. At times it feels as if the focus is getting narrower and narrower as they come at the issue from different angles. On occasions clients will recognise that at some time in the past they have had this conversation with themselves, but now they hear it differently in the presence of another.

The constructivist view that people create meaning for their own lives fosters a climate of experimentation and risk taking in which the counsellor encourages the client to explore different ways of viewing and acting in relation to the problem. This is similar to the personal construct view of the client as a scientist who conducts experiments in living. The counsellor invites the client to share his curiosity as to what might happen next.

It is important that the client feels able to report failure as well as success. Some clients seek the approval of the counsellor and may think that they can only achieve this by reporting good news. This is not helpful because people learn from their mistakes and failures as well as from their successes. The counsellor must ensure that the client feels all his experiences are valid and helpful to the work.

Clients often make progress following an initial interview. This may be due in part to the relief that comes from unburdening one's concerns to another human being. The act of seeking help may in itself restore a sense of power and control in the client's life. Talmon's (1990) research into single sessions demonstrates the power of a first session, showing how it can promote new thinking and behaviour in clients and how, despite the scepticism of many counsellors, it can meet the clients' treatment goals. The solution-focused counsellor sets out to help clients be more aware of how they made changes, however small, and how they might maintain or extend them. If the client reports positive change, the counsellor will offer encouragement and compliments: 'That couldn't have been easy', 'It sounds as if you handled that really well', 'Not many people could have done what you've done', 'How did you manage to do it?' and so on. The delivery of the feedback is as important as the actual content. The manner of delivery will vary according to the personality and circumstances of the client, with a celebratory tone being appropriate in some instances but not in others. It is important for therapeutic momentum that clients accept credit for the changes that they have made and do not attribute progress to the counsellor. The meaning clients attribute to changes they have made will be affected by how pessimistic/optimistic they are; how passive or active; how self-critical/self-affirming; dependent/independent. The pacing and timing of the counsellor's interventions will be affected by these responses.

Clients often feel ambivalent about the changes that they are contemplating or have already made. Change brings losses as well as gains. Some clients choose to live with the status quo because the price of change is too high. Others, in their desperation to escape a painful situation, may make changes that they are unable to sustain or produce short-term benefits but prove destructive in the long term. Some people want cast-iron guarantees that the changes will bring the desired result, while others procrastinate because they are seeking the perfect solution, which of course does not exist.

The counsellor helps clients to consolidate change by asking questions about what is working and how they could maintain or amplify change. These strategies are described in Figure 5.1 under the headings of maintenance, learning and evaluation.

Many clients state that their goal is to have a better understanding of themselves and their problems. Even when they know from experience that better understanding does not guarantee they will be motivated to change or know what or how to change. Understanding can just as easily lead us into justifying the status quo and can become a defence against change. Anyone who has fought against an addiction to food, drugs, cigarettes, alcohol or anything else knows the gap between intellectual conviction and acting on it.

The tenor of the approach is that new awareness can result when clients act differently and that experiential learning is more valuable and powerful than intellectual knowledge: 'learning to be the person you want to be is quite different – and often less time-consuming – than learning why you are the way you are' (Fanger, 1993). We often understand the past more easily by reflecting on the present and the future, than direct historical investigation. However, when a client makes it clear that understanding, for him, is the pre-requisite for constructing solutions, this needs to be respected and co-operated with, otherwise he is likely to lack the motivation to continue.

- *Maintenance strategies*
  What needs to happen for you to keep the changes going? What might stop you from doing that? How will you overcome those obstacles? What would be worth doing again (perhaps in a slightly different way)? (Watzlawick, Weakland and Fisch, 1974). What do you think you need to keep going? What would be the first thing you would do if you saw signs of the problem returning? Who could be on your side to help you with some or all of this?

- *Learning strategies*
  How did you decide to do that (exception)? What do you think that says about you? (White, 1988) What have you learned from what you have tried so far? What have you learned to stop doing? How will you manage to stop yourself doing it again? What will be the gains for you when you abandon your 'failed solutions'? What have you thought about doing instead? How will you be able to remind yourself of what you've learned if the problem arises again? Are there any strategies that you are thinking of experimenting with? Are there some aspects of the problem that you feel you have to live with and others you think you need to change?

- *Evaluation strategies*
  Are you finding these sessions helpful, is it making a difference? Are the changes along the lines that you want? Is your goal the same or has it altered? What should we be doing more or less of? Is there anything else you think it would be helpful to tell me? What else do I need to know in order to help you more?

Figure 5.1 *Counsellor strategies*

Research indicates that the maximum impact of counselling takes place in the first six to eight sessions (Koss and Butcher, 1986). In brief counselling, where time is rationed, there are fewer opportunities to recover from an unproductive start – hence the importance of early and ongoing evaluation by both parties and a willingness on the part of the counsellor to change what she is doing if it is not working. The solution-focused approach is a pragmatic one in which the counsellor experiments with different interventions, depending on whether or not they are helping the client to move towards his goals. If the client is not making progress, they may need to:

- revisit the problem,
- reappraise the client's goals
- re-evaluate the relationship.

Reviewing task performance

Solution-focused counsellors vary in the importance that they attach to offering clients tasks. In the early years of SFT, task-giving occupied a more central role than it does now. The emphasis has moved away from the counsellor prescribing tasks, to supporting clients in tasks that they themselves have designed. Common sense suggests that clients are more likely to make changes that they have initiated themselves than they are those proposed by someone else, although some clients respond to direction from an authority figure. In practice, some clients are less compliant than others and will modify any counsellor suggestion anyway. For example, James was given the task of worrying about his problem for 15 minutes every day in an attempt to reduce the amount of time he wasted worrying about his problems. He carried out the task for three days, then got bored and decided that it would be more productive to spend the time thinking about what he could do to solve his problems. When he reported this to the counsellor, he was congratulated and encouraged to pursue his own ideas about what was most helpful for him.

De Shazer (1996) advises against giving a client another task if he fails to accomplish the one given to him. The counsellor may congratulate the client for knowing that the time was not right to do what had been agreed. The counsellor may ask, 'What did you do instead?' When clients engage in constructive solutions that are different from those agreed in the session, the counsellor will congratulate them on their independent decision. Non-compliance is often a healthy sign! Most counsellors will be delighted when clients design and commit to their own action plan. There is no point in the counsellor advocating a course of action that is unacceptable to the client. The task has to fit the client in his context at this time in his life. Some counsellors work hard to devise clever strategies for clients, only to find that they shrivel up in the cold light of day.

Not all clients feel motivated to engage in between session work. Experience has led them to believe that nothing will make a difference, they have tried everything and nothing works. Their life position is one of passive victimhood or learned helplessness. Yet, resignation to one's fate still requires the ability to cope with the limitations of the situation. In such a case the counsellor will help the client to recognise that she is using coping strategies to stop the situation deteriorating. It could be that doing more of these could even improve it.

Some clients will have received the formula first-session task to do – 'Please notice and come back and tell me things that you would like to see continue in your life' – and so the second session often begins with the client reporting back the answers to this purposefully vague task. The answers often help to redress the problem-centred view of life the client has held up until then.

Constructing solutions

In SFT, the counsellor helps the client to focus in a concrete and detailed way on the various elements in the solution – namely, those changes that the client has stated he wants to bring about. In ongoing work, they collaborate in designing solutions that fit with the client's preferred strategies.

Revisiting the miracle question

Answers to the miracle question change as the work progresses. Clients may decide that one part of the 'miracle' scenario is already happening or that, on reflection, they do not want all, or some aspect, of the miracle.

Predictions

Predictions (Kral and Kowalski, 1989) are quite often utilised in SFT, particularly with clients who report that change happens randomly and cannot, therefore, be repeated. Predictions can help to discover which changes the client would like and how they came about on a particular occasion. The counsellor invites the client to predict each evening whether or not tomorrow is going to be a good or a bad day. At the end of the day, the client checks his prediction for its accuracy. If it was accurate, the client tries to identify what shaped the day. If the prediction was inaccurate, the client might discover the positive experiences that made it a better day than expected or, if the day was worse than predicted, try to identify the trouble spots that might be avoidable in the future, at least to some extent. According to Berg (1991), clients tend, at least initially, to predict more bad days than they actually have. Self-monitoring of predictions can be a valuable learning experience for clients.

Exploring past suggestions

In addition to exploring past solutions, there may be mileage in recalling unused 'solutions'. The reasons for not following these solutions may still be relevant, of course. It may emerge that the suggested course of action was (and still is) a sensible one, but the client was unable to accept it from the person who suggested it. In new circumstances, the client might be willing to revise her earlier decision.

Scaling

In second and subsequent sessions, the counsellor uses scaling questions to monitor progress and set goals. These immensely simple, practical, powerful questions enable the client and the counsellor to be clear about the direction in which the work is going. They ensure that the counsellor stays close to the client's agenda. As in the first session, the use of numbers is a self-regulating activity that the client uses to symbolise his relationship to the problem. It is rare for clients to be unable or unwilling to engage with scaling questions as most experience them as empowering. They convey ownership as it is the client who judges where he is on the scale. The therapist keeps out and does not challenge the client's judgement. Many clients find that scaling their situation makes them feel more hopeful, especially when the emphasis is on making small moves on the scale. It breaks the situation down into small, manageable pieces. Instead of the problem feeling like a mountain, it can be scaled down to a series of climbable hills, with each step plotted along the way. Scaling is a DIY tool that clients can, and frequently do, use between sessions.

At the second session, the counsellor will normally ask the client where she is now on a scale of zero to ten, zero representing either the starting point in counselling or a time when the problem was at its worst and ten a time when the problem has been solved. Clients' initial responses may well be, 'Nothing has changed, everything's the same.' It takes time for some clients to remember what has happened since the last session. Their response is heavily biased towards what has happened in the past day or two, or even the past hour or two. When the counsellor enquires more closely 'Our first session was last Wednesday. How were things on Thursday ... Friday ... Saturday?' the answers become more revealing. With clients who take a pessimistic view of their situation and who tend to report only negative change, the counsellor will ask coping questions, such as, 'It sounds as if you've had a difficult week. How did you get through it? Which was your worst day, which was your second worst day, which was your least worst day?' Scaling discloses variations in the client's situation. It is precisely in this evidence of movement that it becomes possible for the client's 'hidden solutions' to be brought to the surface.

Many skilled and creative practitioners will find ways of illustrating scales in ways that appeal to their clients. Examples I have come across include:

- smiley face at one end, miserable face at the other
- different levels, as in computer games
- a series of mountain peaks
- stepping stones across a river.

EXAMPLE

Client: Friday wasn't too bad.
Counsellor: What was happening on Friday?
Client: I managed to sleep better than I've been doing.
Counsellor: What difference did that make to you during the day?
Client: I was able to work better and I wasn't feeling so down all the time.

Counsellor:	What else was different on Friday?
Client:	Because I wasn't so tired all day, I was in a better mood and I wasn't snapping at my partner all the time.
Counsellor:	So, on a scale of zero to ten, ten being everything was perfect, what were you on Friday?
Client:	Six.
Counsellor:	Would it be all right if you were six every day?
Client:	It would be all right to be six most of the time, but as long as I had some days when I was higher than that – eight or nine.
Counsellor:	What would it take for you to have two days next week that were six?
Client:	Get to bed early and get a good night's sleep would be a start.
Counsellor:	Anything else?
Client:	Make myself some proper meals and cut down on my drinking.
Counsellor:	How could you do that?

Consolidating progress is at least as important as making it in the first place.

EXAMPLE

Client:	I've had a really bad week. I feel like I'm back to square one again.
Counsellor:	So where would you say you were on the scale today?
Client:	Minus five.
Counsellor:	How long do you think you will stay at minus five before you move up or down?
Client:	I don't know. It all depends. If I could only learn to say no when my boss asks me to take on more work, everything would be fine.
Counsellor:	If you managed just once to say no, you think it would make a big difference?
Client:	Yes.
Counsellor:	When will you know that you're ready to move from minus five and start moving up the scale again?
Client:	I'm ready now. I don't want to feel as bad as this again. Things have got to get better.
Counsellor:	What will be the first signs for you that you're beginning to fight back?
Client:	When I stop taking work home with me.
Counsellor:	How could you do that?

The counsellor may also use scaling to find out what the client is doing to stop the situation deteriorating.

EXAMPLE

Counsellor: I know it's been a bad week, but how did you stop it from being even worse?
Client: I went out with my friend on Friday and we had a good talk. It helped me to face Monday. I don't know how I would cope if I couldn't lean on her.
Counsellor: So she's important to you. What else do you do or stop doing when you manage to stop the slide?
Client: I tell myself I'm a lot better than I was a year ago. I know I'm not as much of a doormat as I used to be. I think of all I've been through and survived.
Counsellor: So when you get negative self-critical thoughts, you answer back by remembering how strong you must have been to come through what you did.
Client: Yes.
Counsellor: How do you remind yourself of that?

Clients might report that they are generally better, but not in relation to the problem area itself. They may see no connection between these improvements and the original problem. They may also report that the original problem is solved, but 'things' are still not better. The counsellor will simply stay with the client as they work towards a better understanding of what the client wants.

Developing or reinforcing strategies for change

> If we do not change our direction we are likely to end up where we are headed.
>
> Chinese proverb

The counsellor builds on what the client is doing already to help him take the next small step towards his goal. That step may be towards making further progress, maintaining progress already made or halting further deterioration. What does the counsellor do when clients report no progress or deterioration?

It is important not to focus too much on setbacks. The counsellor may even have warned the client of possible relapses. Failure can provide opportunities for learning. At the very least the client can eliminate one course of action from the list of possible solutions. A relapse or setback can help to throw into clearer relief what the solution might look like. What made the situation worse might give a clue as to what could make it better. The counsellor will try to build on the client's determination not to give up, saying, 'So, despite what has happened you still want to ...?

She may ask:

- 'Do you think that we need to do something different?'
- 'Do you feel our goals are still realistic?'
- 'Do we need to change our timetable?'
- 'How did you manage to stop things getting worse?'
- 'How did you cope despite the problem not improving?'

In some cases, the problem recedes (temporarily or permanently) into the background and something else, either another problem or something positive, comes to the fore. Some clients seem to move from one crisis to another, perhaps needing the adrenalin and sense of being alive that it brings. If one can help the client to identify what it is he gets from such experiences, it may be possible to explore problem-free ways of getting the same thing.

Underestimating the client's capacity for change
As counsellors, we can hold clients back by lacking faith and trust in their ability to make changes in their lives. Although incremental change may most often prove to be a wise course of action, there are occasions when clients are ready for major changes and excessive caution or pessimism on the part of the counsellor can lead to them missing the optimum moment for change. Success often leads to further success.

EXAMPLE

A female client presented at the first session with depression. She was currently off work sick. She felt guilty that she was neglecting her children. When she returned the following week, she had managed to cook a meal for her two children every day after school, had helped them with their homework three times and had visited her place of work to renegotiate her job. The counsellor expressed surprise that she had done so much in one week and asked how she had managed it. Her reply was that she had not intended to do all of these things, but had decided to take control and make a start and one thing had led to another.

Deconstructing the problem

White (1993: 34) defines deconstruction as:

> procedures that subvert taken-for-granted realities and practices: those so-called 'truths' that are split off from the conditions and the context of their production; those disembodied ways of speaking that hide their biases and prejudices; and those familiar practices of self and of relationship that are subjugating people's lives.

There is often a fine line between joining the client in his perceptions and unique experiences of his problem and the necessity at times to explore other interpretations of the situation, other 'truths'. It is not in the spirit of SFT to do this in a confrontational, counsellor as educator way, as one might find in the cognitive therapies. It is more often the case that the worker will help the client to compare times when the problem does not happen with times when it does and, in so doing, clarify the problem itself. The reframing that can emerge from this is more likely to be consistent with the client's own values and viewpoints than would be the case using less collaborative methods.

The self-labelling used by the client is the end product of many years of socially constructed linguistics. The vocabulary adopted is crucially important. While having a diagnosis of an illness can be a source of relief and reassurance in some circumstances, it can also be an albatross around a person's neck. In solution-focused work, the counsellor knows the power language has to construct social reality and is conscious that the language used to describe the 'problem' may be part of the problem. So, the counsellor needs to be aware of the constructions she places on the language that the client uses. She needs to question herself as much as the client and be aware of her motivation in encouraging scepticism about the labels the client has collected.

Being human, we seek to understand our life experiences, although there are times when, as individuals and as a community, meaning eludes us and we are left with mystery. The pace of life in contemporary society and the erosion of traditional political, social and religious beliefs can leave people feeling that they 'had the experience and missed the meaning'. The absence of compelling meaning often lies at the heart of our personal troubles and anxieties. Our desire for meaning and purpose can lead us into a rigid and closed attitude to our experiences, so that we adopt a single filter through which we view the world. This narrowness may prove inadequate in the face of a rapidly changing and challenging environment. Our problems often result from the self-limiting restrictions imposed on our view of life.

As counsellors, we disclose the constructs, assumptions, biases and prejudices that our own belief system is comprised of as it meets the belief system of another human being. Yet, despite these barriers, the purpose of the encounter is to create a bridge between counsellor and client that will enable the client to explore the meaning of his life. Understanding needs to be context-sensitive. In an archaeological dig, the meaning and purpose of a particular artefact can often only be discovered by a careful examination of its location and reference to all the other finds there. If the pattern of relationships has been lost or is unavailable for some reason, the meaning and purpose of the piece becomes obscure. Similarly, in the psychological field, there are choices about meaning that are intrinsically linked to the context of the client's life.

There are various techniques a solution-focused counsellor uses to deconstruct the problem with a client.

Reframing

Reframing provides an alternative perspective on the problem. As Watzlawick, Weakland and Fisch (1974: 95) put it:

> To reframe means to change the conceptual and/or emotional setting or viewpoint in relation to which a situation is experienced and to place it in another frame which fits the 'facts' of the same concrete situation equally well or even better, and thereby changes its entire meaning.

An example of this would be indecision reframed as wise caution. While acknowledging the value of caution, particularly if it compensates for another person's impulsiveness (spontaneity), the counsellor can explore whether or not there are times when the client could allow herself to go off duty and be just a little less cautious for a while.

In the following exchange the two participants negotiate the meaning of crying.

EXAMPLE

Female client: Since she died one thing I've done very little of is actually cry about it. I still don't think I can cry about it and I don't know whether that's odd or I just don't need to, I don't know. People keep telling me I would feel a lot better if I let it all out and there were one or two times I felt I would have liked to have sat down and had a good cry.

Counsellor: Do you usually cry about other things?

Client: No, I don't often cry when I'm upset.

Counsellor: I guess people do what they need to do for themselves. Everyone's different and it might be interesting to think of how you would feel and what you would do differently after you did cry. But I don't feel that you have to think of yourself as needing to do that – 'there must be something wrong with me if I don't cry.' Everyone's different.

From a constructionist perspective, tears have many possible meanings, all of which are negotiable between the two parties. This client holds the dominant cultural belief that she ought to be able to cry about her loss and that she will not get better until she does. She feels anxious and odd because she is unable to cry as other people often do. The counsellor explores the meaning that crying currently occupies in the client's life and offers the view that crying is an option but not a necessity for the client. He suggests that there is no one right way to express feelings. If the client accepts this she may feel released from the obligation to cry and this in turn will break the causal connection between having to cry and her recovery. Learning to cry in what she perceives to be a culturally acceptable way (with strong gender expectations about the place crying occupies in the life of a woman), might be a very difficult thing for her to do and could require a lot of time to accomplish. In the meantime, counselling could be unhelpfully prolonged.

Externalisation
Externalisation of the problem is a form of reframing. It is a way of constructing a therapeutic conversation that locates the problem as being 'out there', not something within the person. It offers a different perspective from which the client can view his problem. Externalising the problem allows the possibility of the person shifting his attitude towards it. The client can, for example, have a greater sense of agency and power whereas previously there was a passive victim stance. Talking about the problem as something that is 'in a relationship with' the client, rather than something the client 'is' or 'has', also changes the counsellor's approach to it. Instead of being the expert who has esoteric knowledge about the inner workings of the client's thoughts and feelings, there is a sense of 'joining with the client' in more of an outward than an inward journey.

EXAMPLE

Frank was subject to recurring bouts of depression. He was convinced that he had been 'hard wired' genetically to be a depressed person, just like his father. His depression was 'something' deep within him. This attitude contributed to a sense of fatalism and hopelessness in the face of this powerful condition. His depression prevented him from valuing anything good about himself or noticing any times when he was less depressed. He was at a loss to explain how he had managed to come out of past depressions. His problem felt like a life sentence. With support, he was eventually able to externalise his depression as a force that attacked him from time to time and overcame him, wrapping its gray blanket of gloom around him. This new way of looking at his feelings opened up new possibilities for:

- learning to recognise the signs of an attack looming
- knowing what he did and can do to defend himself
- knowing what worked in fighting it off or reduced the length or intensity of an attack.

It also helped him to appreciate that there was a lot more to him than his problem. He had strengths, experiences, qualities, values and knowledge that he could utilise more in the fight against the depression. Depression is, of course, a terrible affliction that is not simply shaken off by an act of will power, but how sufferers view it is an important element in their ability to recover from its worst effects.

Externalisation can also help to decrease conflict and blame about ownership of and responsibility for the problem. Without discounting accountability, it is possible to talk about the problem in a way that does not personalise it and thus invite blame, defensiveness and self-justification. It can help couples to face the problem undermining their relationship together. Instead of playing a sterile game of each blaming the other, it can open the door to alternative solutions (White and Epston, 1990).

Testing constructs
The solution-focused counsellor may employ deconstructing strategies used in personal construct counselling. Kelly (1955) advocated a model of the person as a scientist who develops a hypothesis, predicts what might happen, then tests it out and evaluates the results. The counsellor may:

- invite the client to test constructs for their predictive validity or internal consistency
- make more explicit the assumptions on which the constructs are being made
- invite the client to employ a different construct and experiment with it.

The counsellor questions the client's viewing of the problem by commenting on client's thinking as this:

- exaggerates the problem and makes it very difficult to solve
- takes extreme, all-or-nothing positions and leaves little room for compromise or negotiation
- projects responsibility on to others – at some point clients need to become customers for change who take ownership of some aspect of the problem
- sets unrealistic standards by aiming for perfection and dismisses 'good enough' as ever being a viable option
- makes tenuous or illogical connections between events – clients may see two associated events as causally connected.

In SFT, the meaning of each client's experiences is negotiable, depending on the outcome of the linguistic transactions in which the client and therapist engage. The therapist adopts a 'not knowing' position in which she disowns the role of expert in the client's life. The purpose of the therapeutic dialogue is to negotiate jointly a meaning for the client's situation that will create the possibility of change for her. If talking about the problem appears to disempower the client, the therapist averts it by attempting to use other discourses that are potentially more open to change.

- How confident do you feel about following the plan?
- What will you need to keep you to it?
- Which bit do you expect to be the hardest to do?
- What do you think the possible obstacles might be and how will you overcome them?
- What do you need to remember if things get difficult for you again?
- What will be the benefits for you that will make the effort worth it?
- Who is going to be able to help and who do you feel will be part of the problem?
- How long do you think it will take before you feel that this is no longer a big problem?
- How will you remind yourself about the things that you know help?

Figure 5.2   *Questions for ending and after-care*

Evaluating the counselling and planning ending

It is helpful to distinguish between treatment goals and life goals (Ticho, 1972), otherwise counselling can become unduly prolonged. It is not a treatment goal to help a client find a partner or a job, for example, although the treatment goal might be to develop specific social skills in order to achieve that goal. Counselling is the beginning of a process that does not demand the counsellor be there at the end. Figure 5.2 lists a number of questions that focus on how the client could carry forward what she has gained or learned from counselling.

Ending should be on the agenda from the beginning. It should be our aim to remove ourselves from clients' lives as soon as is helpfully possible – as soon as clients are confident that they can carry on the changes they have begun to make. Otherwise there is the danger of dependency and loss of focus in the work. An agency that offers ongoing support to clients has to define it in such a way that it does not become confused with goal-directed counselling.

In SFT, clients define the goals of counselling and largely determine when the contract should end. To some practitioners this will sound like a recipe for long-term work, but for most clients a brief intervention is their treatment of choice. They are more often satisfied with achieving limited, but realistic, goals than are the counsellors.

Scaling is a useful tool for clarifying endings. The counsellor asks the client what will be 'good enough' for him on a scale of zero to ten, with zero being the status quo and ten being the morning after a miracle. She then invites him to describe what will be happening or not happening when he has reached the desired point on the scale. Rarely do clients aspire to being a ten; the most common answers are seven or eight.

It is crucial that there is a clear agreement as to what will constitute the signs for counselling to end. Without such definition, it is difficult to monitor progress. Experience teaches us that endings are not always as clear cut as we would like and there can be differences in perception between the counsellor and the client as to whether or not ending is appropriate. The solution-focused counsellor will always give the client the benefit of the doubt.

In all forms of counselling, endings need preparation and sensitive handling. In brief therapy, when time has been an issue, badly handled endings can leave clients feeling that their problem has been trivialised or they have been written off as beyond help. This can feed into previous negative experiences and leave the client with a devastating sense of failure and rejection.

Long-term work
Although the term solution-focused therapy is often used interchangeably with brief therapy, it should not be identified with it, as there are many other models of brief therapy and SFT can, where needed, be used in long-term work. In such work (over ten sessions), it is crucial to maintain focus and revisit goals. Interventions such as the miracle question and scaling can help to centre the work and ensure that the client's changing agenda is being followed.

Practice points

- Keep the focus on solutions.
- Look for strengths and qualities in the client, even if no apparent progress is being made.
- Use scaling extensively in second and subsequent sessions.
- Use language that opens up possibilities for change.
- In long-term work it becomes even more important to keep the focus on the agenda.
- Keep hopeful, especially when the client isn't.

6

The Solution-focused Practitioner

Anyone who has used the solution-focused approach knows that, although the ideas and interventions are simple to understand, they are not easy to implement – especially when clients do not follow the script! Since the publication of the first edition of this book, this approach has won a huge following from practitioners who do not identify themselves as therapists. They include youth workers and careers advisers, drug and alcohol workers, mentors, social workers, paramedics such as speech therapists, members of youth offending teams and many others. Their specific contexts clearly shape how they adapt the model to meet the needs of their clients, patients, pupils or service users. I am constantly impressed by how creative they are in finding a version of solution-focused language that fits and connects with their clients.

Most practitioners work within an environment where time is limited and there is the pressure of a demanding and heavy caseload. They need to believe that they can do good work when they have only a few (or even a single) sessions with each client. They need to project this conviction to clients who might feel so overwhelmed by their problem that they doubt the helpfulness of a brief or time-limited service. In order to make effective use of time, the practitioner needs to form the working relationship quickly, be skilled in negotiating goals and be disciplined in keeping a focus on the central issue. Certain beliefs or stances help to facilitate this:

- The solution-focused practitioner pays attention to the client's context because it is this that gives meaning to the client's story. What the 'problem' means for the client is on the table for negotiation. The practitioner, taking a non-expert position, will not assume that she can read or interpret the client's situation, nor will she attempt to link a client's 'presenting' problem with a 'deep', hidden, underlying issue. Staying close to the client's stated agenda is a respectful stance that empowers the client and helps to build a collaborative relationship.
- An effective session will usually (but does not always have to) help the client be more aware of his solutions. Hopefully, he will use the time between sessions to implement some of them. Without this active engagement, the momentum for change can disappear, especially when there are limited time and resources, between-session work by the client is essential.

* The solution-focused practitioner's belief that change is always taking place means that it is not up to him to bring about change, but rather to support changes in a direction that is consistent with the client's goals. This fits with the solution-focused minimalist philosophy of doing more with less. The practitioner is part of the problem-solution system and has an influence on whether the work is brief or long term.

Becoming an effective solution-focused practitioner

There is no formula for success, as the individuality of each person will shape the solution-focused relationship. However, there seem to me to be a number of skills or qualities required (see Figure 6.1).

• Attentiveness	• Acceptance
• Discipline	• Genuineness
• Warmth	• Empathy
• Curiosity	• Humour

Figure 6.1   *Skills and qualities of a solution-focused practitioner*

* Attentiveness involves active listening, which means hearing and mirroring the client's language and imagery. One element of attentiveness is noting the client's body language. Being solution-focused entails being 'present with' the client and attending to the 'here and now' interaction in the room.
* Discipline in listening and responding to the client. A disciplined focus keeps the session on solution-track and does not allow it to be diverted into problem 'dead ends'. For counsellors trained in a problem-focused approach, resist the voice in your head directing you to investigate and analyse the problem aspects of the client's story. Additionally, a solution-focused practitioner needs a sense of timing to know when to assist the client to move from problem-talk to solution-talk. Kiser, Piercy and Lipchik (1993: 235) state, 'The movement in SFT from problems to solutions is not automatic. It involves considerable therapeutic skill to help a client move from feeling bad and talking about negative experiences to feeling bad and shifting focus to more positive emotions.' Clients vary a great deal in their need to expand on the problem and their ability to explore strategies to make it better. The effective practitioner will pace himself to meet the needs of each client. The counsellor needs good powers of concentration and memory and an ability to give the client succinct, balanced summaries of exceptions and successes. It can be helpful to take notes during the sessions. Without

notes, it is difficult to remember answers to the miracle or scaling questions. Noting solution-talk and exceptions to the problem also reinforces the importance of these steps towards solutions.

- Warmth, patience, tenacity, tact and curiosity are needed in order to enter the client's frame of reference in a respectful, non-intrusive manner. A relentless form of questioning can make the client feel pressurised into giving the kind of answer she thinks he wants. The skilled counsellor will break the question–answer cycle by making empathic and reflective interventions. The curiosity he shows will be about the client's resources and solutions, not about their problems.

- Acceptance, genuineness and empathy are core conditions of a solution-focused, client-centred relationship. It is crucial that the client feels safe and accepted. For the client to feel blamed or criticised is incompatible with solution-focused principles.

- Humour can be therapeutic in itself. Some of the interventions used in the solution-focused approach naturally lead to amusing conversations. A light touch can be therapeutic. There are times when it is helpful to laugh at ourselves and become aware of our absurdities.

In a way, it is easier for counsellors to like or respect their clients when the conversation is more about their solutions than their problems. If the interview is preoccupied with problems to the exclusion of validating the client's resources, then it is hardly surprising that clients often feel pessimistic following such a session.

In SFT, the task of the counsellor is not to uncover the lost 'truth' that will explain the client's current problems – the 'counsellor as psychological detective' model – but, rather, create a climate in which people have a voice to express their experience and have their strengths and competence affirmed. This is often denied those whose view of the world is usually devalued, marginalised or suppressed by virtue of their sex, race, culture, sexual orientation or disability. The solution-focused postmodern perspective supports pluralism and diversity in thinking and action.

The solution-focused process

The following account of a real example of work with a client highlights many of the points made throughout the book.

The client was a white female in her forties, married, with three children. She had a well-paid, white-collar job and had to work long hours while juggling childcare and responsibilities regarding her elderly mother. Her husband often worked away from home.

Approximately two years prior to coming for counselling, she had felt 'on the verge of a nervous breakdown' and had had to take time off work. She had returned to work after three months and renegotiated a less stressful role in the company.

However, she had begun to experience similar stress-related symptoms again and, immediately prior to coming for counselling, had taken sick leave. She described herself as being anxious, indecisive and short-tempered at home, particularly with the children. Her memory and concentration were poor and she was not sleeping well. During the first session the client talked at length about her problems at home and work, although she said she had felt unsure about doing so. The counsellor validated the client's feelings and experiences, while listening for examples of coping strategies. He asked the miracle question and received an answer that included noticing she would:

- be sleeping better
- be feeling mentally calmer
- be more supported by her husband
- play with her children and not shout at them
- be back at work and able to cope with the pressures without being snappy and making mistakes.

The counsellor asked, 'On a scale of zero to ten, ten representing the morning after the miracle and zero the worst you've ever been, where would you put yourself today? The client answered that she was at three. At the end of the session the counsellor invited the client to notice times when she managed to control her worry habit even a little and remember what she did to achieve that. She was also asked to write down a list of things that she thought she could do in order to reduce her stress levels. The client appeared motivated and keen to use the time off work to 'sort herself out'.

When she returned for the second session, the counsellor asked, 'What's better?' She described situations when she felt free from stress – gardening, going out with her friend to an evening class, reading, taking her children to the cinema. In the feedback the counsellor gave her, he congratulated her on what she had managed to do. In terms of utilising her skills and experience, the counsellor noted that she had a lot of energy and was creative and caring in her approach to the problem. The counsellor reminded her that she had overcome this problem before and wondered if she could remember anything that had worked the last time. She felt that her husband had been very supportive then and she needed him to support her more at the moment.

During the third session, the client reported that she was surprised (as was her husband) at how well she was doing.

Client:	I've been able to think about going back to work without it waking me up in the middle of the night.
Counsellor:	How did you manage to do that?
Client:	I think I've come to see that there's more to life than just working all the time. I've begun to stand back from it.

The client had begun to change how she viewed her problem. The counsellor invited her to continue doing what was working and think through the implications of her new way of looking at her job.

At the fourth session, she reported that she found scaling helpful and used it each day to measure how she had dealt with particularly stressful situations. She felt calmer, more relaxed and had stopped 'flying' at her daughter. She was experimenting with taking small manageable steps towards controlling her anxiety.

She reported that she was six on the scale. She was sleeping better and had come to realise that things would never be perfect. She would be happy to achieve a seven, not a ten. The counsellor affirmed the client's self-awareness and problem-solving strategies and reinforced her repertoire by expressing the view that, once acquired, these skills would not be lost, as long as they were consolidated by regular practice. The counsellor also suggested that skills used in the domestic arena were transferable to the work environment. This belief helped to increase the possibility that the counselling could be effective and brief.

> *Counsellor*: I've seen you make progress and there's every reason to believe that you can maintain that. I know that people can transfer these skills. I think it's important to realise that it's basically the same stuff. It's just a different place or environment. You've got the tools there. You're doing the job already.

By the sixth session, the client felt she was handling relationships at home much better, but felt anxious about the impending return to work. Despite her apprehension, she had developed a 'survival plan' for her first few weeks back. Her solutions included a determination to say 'No' to extra work, a request for a meeting with her boss to negotiate extra resources and avoidance of any unnecessary travel. In the feedback to the client, the counsellor complimented her on her self-care skills and her courage in facing up to a stressful situation. The client sought reassurance that the counselling could continue for a few more weeks until she felt more confident about work.

In the next session, the client said that she felt she had had a setback and felt quite depressed about work. She had visited her workplace, but had felt overwhelmed and her colleagues had not been very friendly. The counsellor reassured her that 'practising new habits is often bumpy'. He also explored how she was managing to stop things getting worse. Her answer was the increased support at home.

In the final two sessions, the client revisited the miracle question and applied it to her work situation – looking at how colleagues would be treating her, the amount and kind of work she would be doing and so on. She recognised that she had 'moved down a gear' and was more in control. She liked her 'new self'. After nine sessions, she felt that she had learnt sound strategies for handling her stress and decided to end counselling. Her closing comments were:

I've noticed that everything seems to be looking forwards. It seems to be a lot more realistic. You don't waste a lot of time. It's not just a case of someone listening to you, it's doing something about it, and what I've noticed is that in a conversation you've said to me, 'How was your week? How did you rate your week?' Now I know next week you'll probably ask me the same question, so you make me really accountable. I feel as though I'm sitting here talking about how my week's been, then suddenly you'll sort of pull it forward. The first time it took my breath away. I felt after it a great sense of achievement. This is a good way to go. This is a nice way.

This account typifies many solution-focused conversations.

- The two work collaboratively within the client's frame of reference, utilising her motivation, energy and imagination.
- The counsellor supports the client's decisions and experiments as she works towards her goals.
- They look for exceptions, engage and scale progress.
- They use the past as evidence of the clients' resources and transferable skills.
- The emphasis is on focusing more on the future than the past.
- The counsellor openly compliments the client on the helpful actions she is taking. It is empowering for clients to be given credit for success, particularly if they see themselves as being inadequate or out of control. However, it is not always easy for people to accept and own their achievements and there is little to be gained by the counsellor trying to persuade clients that they have achieved more than they are willing to own. Practitioners need to be aware that clients may be anxious that help will be withdrawn if they acknowledge that they are coping better.
- The counselling ends when the client is confident that she can maintain progress. This does not preclude the natural anxiety on both sides that can accompany endings. The counsellor will leave the door open for the client to return if necessary.
- The client has become her own counsellor.

Counsellor interventions

In an analysis of four transcripts of solution-focused conversations, O'Connell(1997) identified specific categories of counsellor interventions. Some of these were to build rapport, such as:

- encouragement
- giving support
- agreement prompts
- joint completion of client sentences
- use of humour
- validation of clients' experiences
- normalisation statements.

Empathy in the interviews focused on what the client was already doing/ thinking/feeling in order to solve the problem. The 'getting alongside', supportive approach was a conscious strategy to build a co-operative, collaborative relationship. Building rapport helped to motivate clients towards solutions and took place throughout the sessions, even when the main focus had shifted to strategies and action plans.

Joint completion of clients' sentences was a deliberate therapeutic strategy (Gale and Newfield, 1992), designed to increase the clients' trust by demonstrating the accuracy and empathy of the counsellor's listening and understanding.

Other interventions were more clearly related to exploring the themes of change, solution and strategy:

- change-talk
- solution-talk
- strategy-talk.

Change-talk
In change-talk, a key theme is seeking difference. When the clients talked about problem or solution events, the counsellor attempted to find, in Bateson's phrase, 'the difference that makes the difference' (1972).

The counsellor used circular questions to discover the impact that an event had on the clients and other significant people. The ability to notice difference in the problem situation injected fluidity and dynamism into what otherwise felt like a fixed and rigid pattern to the clients.

Solution-talk
The focus of solution-talk was on constructing the future that the client wanted. The counsellor used pre-suppositional questions, the principal of which was the miracle question.

EXAMPLE

Counsellor: Let me ask you a question, Tom, that we often ask people. It's an unusual question, but people often find it very helpful. If you woke up tomorrow and somehow things were better, what would be the first things you would notice?

Client: I think if I woke up and felt like I did 20 years ago, then I'd feel that must have been a miracle.

Counsellor: So, what would be different for you that day?

Client: Life would be a lot slower. I think life is too fast anyway, but with me I make it even faster.

Counsellor: So what would you be doing more slowly after the miracle?

Client:	I'd get up at the right time to go to the day centre. At the moment I get up too early and worry about getting there when I don't need to. It's part of my anxiety. I worry about everything.
Counsellor:	So, if a miracle happened, you wouldn't be worried about so many things.
Client:	No. I'd have a clear mind, I'd be remembering things better and my concentration would be better.
Counsellor:	What else would be different for you?
Client:	I'd be able to relax more. I'd be able to plan ahead, maybe what I want to do tomorrow or next week. Then think to myself I've to go all out and do it. Whereas now I say I'm going to do things but I don't bother to do them. I think if the miracle happened I'd try to look on the positive side of things. At the moment I look very much on the negative side. I'd start enjoying life.
Counsellor:	And that's something you'd very much like.
Client:	Yes. I've always enjoyed mixing with people. I go to the club on Tuesdays, the people are great. I can laugh and joke if I'm not feeling too bad. I leave there and as soon as I get back to the house I'm a different person. When I'm in company I'm a different person.
Counsellor:	So, after the miracle, will you be spending more time with other people or more time on your own?
Client:	I'd sooner be among other people, but not big crowds, I couldn't stick that. If I had a good social life, going back to my house each day, I could relax. I'm sure I could. I could watch the box and have a good night's sleep. I think I'd be 95 per cent there, I'm sure I would.

Strategy-talk

Strategy-talk was conversation that related to what the client was already doing or planning to do about managing the problem. It took place more towards the end of interviews than at the beginning, but was present throughout. Forms of strategy talk included:

- *Coping questions*
  Here the counsellor elicited from the client how he had managed to cope, despite all the difficulties. On other occasions, the counsellor recognised that the client was already working on problem-solving strategies and facilitated him in extending his repertoire.
- *Multiple-choice questions*
  When exploring strategies, on occasions the counsellor asked the client multiple-choice questions about available strategies. In this example the counsellor pre-empted unhelpful strategies, while at the same time suggesting that the client had, or might have, found other ways of tackling the problem.

> *Counsellor*: So what do you do? Do you jump up and go into total panic or go and do 50 things about it? Do you talk to someone or do you deal with it differently?
>
> *Client*: Well, I mean there's two ways I've found that I ...

This may be viewed by the client as making suggestions, but the counsellor sees it as a vehicle for promoting giving clients choices.

* *Scaling questions*
  These were used to measure confidence, motivation and progress and are described more fully in Chapter 4.

Practice points

* Pay attention to the client's context.
* Our role is not to change clients, but to help clients be more aware of how positive change is already happening and how they could encourage it.
* Practice increased awareness of solutions.
* Help clients find 'the difference that makes the difference.'
* Think carefully about the timing for moving from problem- to solution-talk.
* Remember that solution-focused ideas are simple, but putting them into practice takes skill and sensitivity.

7

Solution-focused Supervision

The Ethical Framework (2003), laid down by the British Association for Counselling and Psychotherapy states:

> All counsellors, psychotherapists, trainers and supervisors are required to have regular and ongoing formal supervision/consultative support for their work in accordance with professional requirements. ... It is important to be open to, and conscientious in considering, feedback from colleagues, appraisals and assessments.

Not all the helping professions place such a strong emphasis on the need for all practitioners – no matter how experienced or well qualified – to receive ongoing supervision for their work. There is, however, an increasing move in this direction among organisations where staff interact with the general public. They recognise the dual importance of showing due care for their employees and protecting vulnerable members of the public.

The term 'supervision' is perhaps an unfortunate one, open to misunderstanding by outsiders to the counselling profession. Supervision does not mean that the supervisor has 'super vision' and can see things that the supervisee can't! Nor does it imply that supervisees are still in training or are inexperienced and need to be managed and directed in their work. A more egalitarian term such as 'consultation' better describes the relationship.

A solution-focused model of supervision clearly mirrors the values and practices of the therapeutic model itself. In its original context of family therapy, supervision took a very specific form. Therapists received live 'supervision' from colleagues, who observed their interviews from behind a two-way mirror. This supportive learning, which, on occasions, included the client, reduced the need for individual supervision. It is this open, team approach that explains the apparent lack of interest from the founders of the approach in one-to-one supervision. Their collaborative style of supervision and group reflection was immediate and powerful. It encouraged transparency of practice. However, in this country at least, there are many solution-focused practitioners who do not work in such an environment and receive only one-to-one supervision, if they receive any at all. Those who work in a counselling capacity *without* having regular consultations or supervision are working unethically.

Building on competence

Solution-focused supervision validates the competence and resources of the supervisee, emphasises the importance of clear, incremental goals and identifies pre-existing solutions and exceptions to problems in the supervisee's work. It focuses more on what the supervisee is doing than on client issues directly. It attends to process from an interactional perspective rather than from an intra-psychic one.

In solution-focused supervision, the supervisor regards the supervisee as essentially competent, skilled and cooperative. Wetchler (1990) describes the role of the supervisor as concentrating on what the supervisee is doing effectively and assisting the supervisee in continuing to do those things. In solution-focused supervision there is a clear contract that identifies learning goals for the supervisee based on his or her current level of professional development (Selekman and Todd, 1995).

Supervisors occupy a powerful role as gatekeepers to their profession and, as with any organisation, there can be a tendency to admit people who 'are one of us'. In the solution-focused community, however, there is an inbuilt resistance to orthodoxy and a desire to respect diversity in practice. There is a postmodern uneasiness about gurus and self-styled 'guardians of the faith' and a wish to be as inclusive as possible when it comes to membership. It resists styles of supervision and rules of membership that debar creative, talented people because they have not jumped through the hoops demanded by the Establishment. This requires a respect for difference and trust in the supervisees.

Supporting expertise

Solution-focused supervision is less hierarchical and more collegial than many traditional forms of supervision. Thomas (1994) describes the supervisor as 'coaxing the expertise' out of the supervisee, rather than being a dispenser of wisdom. The supervisor fosters an atmosphere of mutual respect in which both parties celebrate skills, creative ideas, personal qualities and therapeutic successes. Supervision is an 'inventive art' (Cantwell and Holmes, 1995). Curiosity – an attitude encouraged in solution-focused therapy (SFT) – prompts the supervisor to find out how best to co-operate uniquely with this supervisee. The exploration will encompass the supervisee's own preferred learning styles, use of language, prior experience of supervision, stage of professional development, personal qualities and context.

Supervision is essentially a collaborative partnership in which both sides take responsibility for negotiating the goals and options available. In practice, the balance of collaboration will vary according to the level of expertise and experience of the supervisee.

The 'one down' position

The supervisor adopts a 'one down' position in order to learn from the supervisee which supervisory style works for him. The supervisor, in Cantwell and Holmes' (1995) phrase, 'leads from one step behind'. In practice, this means that the supervisor does not assume the role of expert in all matters, but, rather, seeks to validate expertise in the supervisee. Taking a 'one down' position opens up space for new learning and challenges the supervisee to explore unfamiliar territory. Dialogue becomes the primary paradigm of the relationship. This stance will be consistent with the supervisor's duty of care towards clients, whereby she upholds the norms of good practice and ethical behaviour. Her responsibility will require that she challenges any unprofessional conduct and takes active steps to stop unsafe practices. Counsellors sometimes need to be protected from themselves.

The solution-focused supervisor demonstrates good listening skills and is able to use reflective silences purposefully. The respectfulness of the 'one down' position helps to reduce the possibility of unintentional oppressive practice. This can easily arise given the range of differences potentially present between supervisor and supervisee, such as age, gender, race, class, beliefs, sexual preference and disability.

From a constructivist standpoint, supervision is a mutual social construction in which the meaning of language is negotiated within a specific context (Anderson and Swim, 1995). There is an understanding that there is no 'one truth' about either the sessions themselves or, indeed, about the supervision sessions. There are multiple realities, voices to be heard, contexts to be respected. The supervisor will draw the supervisee's attention to the way in which she uses language to describe realities 'out there' as if they had independent objectivity. This sensitivity towards language can help to make the supervisee think carefully about the ways in which she shapes the client's problem and deals with it. It can also open up rich possibilities for understanding the many meanings that clients attach to events in their lives.

Supervision is a 'parallel process' to work with clients. If, for example, a counsellor reports that she is having a problem in helping a client to find ways forward, the supervisor will use solution-focused interventions, such as the miracle question, to help the supervisee find ways forward in her work. Supervision thus becomes reflective experiential learning.

The solution-focused supervisor will model the techniques of the approach as well as its values and beliefs. The techniques include:

- exception seeking
- giving credit to the supervisee
- the miracle question
- scaling.

EXCEPTION SEEKING

In the following example, the supervisee had succeeded in gaining the confidence of an initially suspicious and cautious client.

Supervisee: It was very hard going for the first few weeks. There were long silences that didn't feel very productive. I felt as if she was testing me out. When I started to offer suggestions, she always had some reason for not being able to do anything.

Supervisor: So things got a bit easier after the first few sessions? How did that happen?

Supervisee: I stopped making suggestions, so I felt less frustrated. I told her that many people would not have coped as well as she had done. I began to compliment her on the way she was thinking about the problem and said that she would know when to do something about it.

Supervisor: It sounds as if, once you made fewer demands on her and took a more positive view, you began to get on better with her.

Supervisee: It was really strange how the less I tried to push, the more she seemed to come out of her shell. I think she was amazed at me complimenting her.

Supervisor: Your approach seems to have opened a few doors for her. Some therapists might have been tempted to batter the door down, but you seemed to sense that it was better to back off and give her some space. Is that something you intend to continue and perhaps do more of?

The supervisor invites the supervisee to recall those times when she managed, if only temporarily, to do something different with the client that was successful. Exception seeking breaks the problem cycle and provides evidence of times when the supervisee was not so 'stuck' (from a solution-focused perspective being stuck is not in fact possible, as everyone is constantly in a process of interactive change). Rather than analysing why the work with the client felt stuck (which could lead to a long speculative exploration), the supervisor helps the supervisee to reflect on those exceptions when the feeling of being stuck was not there or not there to the same degree.

• What was happening on those occasions? Who said what? How?
• What made the difference? How did it make a difference?
• How could you do this again or more often?

GIVING CREDIT TO THE SUPERVISEE

Practitioners need to have their therapeutic skills validated and due credit given for good practice, as they in turn give clients credit for their successes. They need to know what they did well and how they did it in order to be able to reproduce it. Solution-focused supervision sessions are likely to begin with the question, 'What did you feel you succeeded in doing with this particular client?' (Merl, 1995). Identifying competence is more likely to increase professional confidence than a pre-occupation with deficits and mistakes. If supervisees can come to believe that, essentiallty, they are competent, they are more likely to be receptive to new learning and more willing to experiment in their practice than if the focus is constantly on their mistakes or faults. They may also then accept that mistakes are permissible and present opportunities for valuable learning. Practitioners who are clear about their strengths and limitations are more likely to work within their competence, as stated in their professional Codes of Ethics and Practice.

THE MIRACLE QUESTION

The supervisor may use the miracle question – 'If you were working better with this client and your current difficulties had been overcome, what would be the first signs for you that a miracle had happened?'

Supervisee: My heart wouldn't sink when I saw him in the waiting room.

Supervisor: After the miracle, how would you be feeling and what would you be thinking when you saw him there?

Supervisee: I would smile at him the way I do with most clients and sound a bit more enthusiastic in asking him to come in.

Supervisor: What else?

Supervisee: When he started talking, he would let me get a word in edgeways, rather than just launching into a verbal attack, as he usually does.

Supervisor: What difference would that make to you?

Supervisee: I'd feel that I had something to offer rather than just being a dumping ground for all his complaints, without him being willing to let me help him change.

Supervisor: What else would be happening once the miracle had happened?

Supervisee: I wouldn't be feeling so weary and hopeless after seeing him.

Supervisor: How would you be feeling at the end of a session?

Supervisee: I would feel that he had worked harder than me and that it was worthwhile trying to help him.

Supervisor: If you were to bring this client to supervision three months from now and you were telling me that things were much better, how would it have come about? What would have happened to make it happen?

Supervisee: I would have found ways of keeping him on the subject and listening to what *I* have to say for a change.

Supervisor: I wonder how you would have managed to do that?

Supervisee: I would have an agreed agenda for a session and interrupt him once he went off on a tangent. I also think that I would have given him things to do between sessions and started off a session by asking him whether he'd done them or not. I think if I could get him to keep to the point most of the time I wouldn't mind if occasionally he went off on a monologue.

Supervisor: So you would have more of a structure to the session than you have at the moment?

Supervisee: I think that I would have limited the sessions to less than an hour as well. Then I wouldn't feel so drained at the end of them. I think I could do a better job with him in half an hour than in an hour.

Supervisor: That sounds as if you are thinking of ways that will help you to be more effective and look after yourself at the same time. How will you do this in a way that impacts positively on your client?

The miracle question encourages supervisees to talk about improving their practice without feeling that they have to defend or justify themselves. The future orientation reduces the possibility of them feeling discouraged or de-skilled by past failures. Providing that the supervisor moves at the right pace, the miracle question should not raise unrealistic expectations, but it will relate closely to the supervisees' current level of expertise.

SCALING

Scaling is often used in solution-focused supervision to develop answers to the miracle question, but it can also be used at other times. The supervisor would ask the following kinds of questions:

- On a scale of zero to ten, ten being your effectiveness with this client after the miracle and zero the lowest it's ever been, where would you say you are today?
- Where would you like to get to?
- What would it look like when you got there?
- What would be happening that's not happening at the moment?
- What would have stopped happening?
- What would need to happen for that to happen?
- What would be the first thing that you would do?
- What would the client notice was different?
- What would you need to remind yourself about?
- If there were setbacks, how would you get back on track?

The supervisor may ask scaling questions in relation to the supervisee's confidence or motivation to work more effectively with this client. Some solution-focused supervisors prefer to ask their supervisee where the *client* would scale the work rather than the supervisee herself – the rationale being that practitioners usually rate their work lower than their clients do. Personally, my experience does not confirm that. I have met a number of counsellors who rate themselves more generously than others might! The following are the sorts of questions that a supervisor would ask in this area.

- On a scale of zero to ten, zero being the lowest and ten being the highest, how confident are you that you can improve your work with this client?
- Is that good enough for you to make a start?
- If not, where would you need to get to for that to happen?

- What would be the first step for you towards building up your confidence?
- What would your client notice was different about you?

In terms of motivation to change, the supervisor uses the same scale and follows it up with the following supplementary questions.

- Is that motivation level high enough for you to make a start?
- If not, where do you need to get to?
- How could you move one point on the motivation scale?
- How would the client experience your new motivation?
- If things were to improve with this client, how would this affect your work with other clients?
- How would this improvement affect your level of job satisfaction?

There is a legitimate place for encouragement and compliments from the supervisor on what she is doing well. The restorative function of supervision is very important (Inskipp and Proctor, 1989). Supervision should recharge the batteries and stimulate the brain cells.

Goals

Solution-focused work stresses the importance of negotiating specific outcomes. Both parties monitor whether or not clear and realistic goals are being set with the client and if progress is being made towards achieving them.

Perhaps one of the most useful ways in which a solution-focused approach can help supervisees is that of focusing on endings. It aims to have a sense of ending from the beginning. This decreases the chances of work finishing abruptly or drifting. Using a scaling question, for example, might reveal that the client expects the work to finish when he moves from two to five. Supervision may then illuminate how the supervisee could keep this expectation in mind, recognise the signs along the way and stop when the client feels confident that she is heading in the right direction.

To summarise, solution-focused supervision is a respectful and creative activity that calls on many of the interventions used in the client work itself. It is competence-based and future-orientated. It stays close to the supervisee's agenda without sacrificing the ethical and professional responsibilities of the supervisor.

Solution-Focused One-to-One Supervision

A five-stage model
Although I hesitate to describe something as a staged process, as it can easily be turned into a mechanical set of routines, a structure can help to

clarify what happens. The structure shown in Figure 7.1 and described in the text that follows outlines a possible beginning, middle and end to a solution-focused supervision session.

Stage 1: Negotiate session goals
Stage 2: Working with the supervisees' strengths and solutions
Stage 3: Future thinking
Stage 4: Scaling progress
Stage 5: Ending

Figure 7.1   *The Supervision Process*

STAGE 1: NEGOTIATE SESSION GOALS
The primary focus in the supervision is on the practitioner in relation to the client, not on the client himself. For the supervision to be most effective, it is desirable for the supervisee and the supervisor to have agreed beforehand how they want to use the session. Some opening questions from the supervisor may include versions of the following.

- What do you hope to gain from this session today?
- How will you know that it has been worthwhile?
- What needs to happen to make sure that this session is helpful for you?
- What difference do you hope this will make to your work with clients?

In keeping with the parallel process of the work itself, the supervisor will ask about pre-session change – for example, 'In the time leading up to this session, have there been any changes in the situations we wanted to discuss today?'

STAGE 2: WORKING WITH THE SUPERVISEE'S STRENGTHS AND SOLUTIONS
The supervisor enquires about the supervisee's competence and facilitates an exploration of how she could do more of what works. The focus is on the supervisee, not the client.

- Which skills does this client elicit from you?
- What are you doing well with this client?
- What do you think this client likes about the way you work with her?
- What does your client find helpful?
- How could you do more of it?
- (If there are difficulties) Have you ever come across a similar situation with this or another client?
- What happened then that was helpful?
- Could any of that be helpful now?
- What keeps you hopeful about this client?

STAGE 3: FUTURE THINKING

The supervisor may use the miracle question, as described before, and develop the answers by asking the following kinds of questions.

- What else would you notice? What else? What else? ...
- What skill or quality did the miracle bring you?
- Have there been any times recently with this client when some of the miracle happened?
- What would need to happen for this to happen again or for longer?

It is important to remember that the miracle happened to the worker, not the client, so the changes may not be immediately evident in the client. However, if the worker changes, there is always the possibility that the client may change as well.

STAGE 4: SCALING PROGRESS

Scaling can be helpful at any point of the supervision process, but may naturally flow from answers to the miracle question.

- If ten is that you are doing a good job with this client, given all the circumstances, and zero is that you are doing the complete opposite, where do you think your client would put you?
- Where would you put yourself?
- How could you move up one point on the scale?
- If you could only do one thing differently with this client, what would it be?

STAGE 5: ENDING

The supervisor will give the supervisee feedback about how he came over in the session itself, as well as highlighting what the supervisee is doing that is helpful with the client.

- I [the supervisor] would just like to say how impressed ... how struck ... how much I appreciated ... what you did/said ... here today.
- I liked the way you handled ... with your client.

The supervisor may pass the job of ending the session over to the supervisee.

- Could you sum up what you are taking away from today's session?
- How has this been helpful to you?
- What will you try to do differently?
- Is there anything else we need to discuss before we finish?

Team Supervision and Peer Support

Drawing on the Reflecting Team model developed by Norman (2003) and others, I have found the following framework very popular with staff who wish to offer peer group support or supervision. Keeping to the structure is important as the focused discipline of it seems to be the key to its success.

The 'Presenter' brings an issue or piece of client work to the team to sound out their ideas. The 'Process Manager' is appointed to ensure that members keep to the sequence of stages. A 'Timekeeper' keeps the team to the time allocated to each stage. The optimum number is seven, with four as a minimum and ten as a maximum. Most teams find that sitting in a circle, preferably around a table, encourages people to make contributions.

As well as carrying out their roles, the Process Manager and Timekeeper contribute to the discussion.

Members are encouraged to listen to and build on what others have said, rather than concentrate on their own statements or questions. As it is a solution-focused meeting, the contributions are informed by the values and interventions central to SFT.

Running a Reflecting Team

To a considerable extent, a Reflecting Team runs itself and, when teams have used it over a period of time, minimal formality may be enough. However, until the team is happy with its own style, keeping to the roles, stages, time and ground rules is recommended.

THE PROCESS MANAGER (PM)

The role of the Process Manager (PM) is to help members keep to the correct sequence of stages and assist the Presenter in making the session useful for himself and the others. Where possible, a preparatory meeting between the PM and the Presenter is helpful. In her contributions to the discussion the PM can model interventions to the rest of the group by, for example, building on what others have said. If members of the team are easily distracted from the topic or want to prolong discussion after the conclusion, the PM has to be the one who keeps them on track or brings the session to an end. Most solution-focused practitioners will be positive and supportive in their contributions, but if there is anyone who takes a superior or critical line, he or she needs to be reminded by the PM that the group is looking for strengths to build on, not weaknesses to attack.

THE PRESENTER

To some extent the success of the session depends on the quality of the presentation. It is therefore important for the Presenter to use the time well by thinking about the main points she wants to make and not getting bogged down in unnecessary case detail. Keeping the focus on the work, not on the client, is helpful.

Some of the best presentations I have seen have been when the Presenter has been non-defensive and genuinely asking for ideas from colleagues. A vulnerability on her part usually brings out supportive contributions from colleagues. For me, the rule about the Presenter only listening, not speaking, during the Reflection stage is one of the most helpful aspects of the format.

TEAM MEMBERS
As the reflecting team is a mutual learning forum, it requires members to listen to and learn from one another. The rule about building on each other's ideas helps to build respect, team identity and spirit. The hope is that the interest in and support for one another's work will continue outside of the meetings.

PREPARATION
Preparation is the first step (see Figure 7.2).

The Process Manager discusses with the Presenter what the focus of the session will be. In well-prepared teams, members will have received a brief summary of the issue and specific requests for help from the Presenter. It has to be made clear to team members that the focus is on their colleague, not on the absent client.

> **Preparation**
> **Presentation**
> **Clarification**
> **Affirmation**
> **Reflection**
> **Conclusion**

Figure 7.2 *Six-step framework for Team Supervision*

PRESENTATION (5 MINUTES)
Only the Presenter speaks. S/he gives the team the background to the issue or describes the work done to date.

CLARIFICATION (7 MINUTES)
The members of the team, asking one question each in turn, seek to clarify the situation. Questions masking advice are ruled out of order! The Process Manager ensures that no one dominates and everyone has the opportunity to speak. If an individual cannot think of a question, s/he simply says 'Pass'. Solution-focused questions about a piece of work may include the following.

- Has there been a time when you feel that you have been more effective with this client? (Exception seeking)
- What do you like about what you have done with this client? (Seeking competence).
- What do you think your client would say s/he valued about your input?
- If a miracle happened overnight in the way you worked with this client, but as you were asleep you would not have known, what would be the first signs for you that a miracle had happened?
- If this miracle had given you a particular gift or quality that would be really useful with this client, what would it be and how would it make a difference?
- On a scale of zero to ten, with ten being that you are doing your absolute best with this client, where would you put yourself at the moment?
- If you did one thing in the next week or two to improve things, what would it be?
- What would need to happen for that to occur?

AFFIRMATION (3 MINUTES)
Each member in turn pays a compliment to the Presenter about the content and manner of the presentation. The Presenter simply accepts the feedback. Members may indicate their agreement with the opinions of others in the group.

REFLECTION (12 MINUTES)
The members of the team take turns to share their thoughts about the issue. They do this by raising or answering questions with the Presenter remaining silent. Instead, s/he listens and takes notes of what the group says.

The team remains true to the solution-focused spirit by building on the Presenter's strategies and views, rather than taking a 'cleverer-than-thou' position. The team tries to give the Presenter what s/he asked for – in most cases, it will be some new ideas about how to work with the client.

CONCLUSION (3 MINUTES)
The conclusion belongs to the Presenter, with no one else speaking. S/he thanks the team members for their ideas and then summarises what s/he is taking from the session – mentioning specific things that s/he is going to think about further or do.

When the Presenter has finished, so has the session. In total, the session will have taken approximately 30 minutes. There is no further discussion, unless it has been agreed that the team will discuss, for a specified time, general issues arising from the session. It can be helpful, for example, for each person to say how she or he benefited from the discussion and how it might improve their work.

WHAT COLLEAGUES IDENTIFY AS MOST VALUABLE ABOUT THIS FORMAT

- It focuses the discussion.
- It prevents the voluble members of the team from dominating the discussion and enables the more reticent to contribute.
- It is affirming and respectful to the Presenter.
- It allows the Presenter to share his or her work without being defensive.
- It is a good teaching forum for everyone, not only the Presenter.
- It strengthens the team's identity.
- It is a model for discussion that can also be used with clients.

Conclusion

Solution-focused values and interventions can make one-to-one and group supervision a life-enhancing experience for those participating. When done well, it sends supervisees out enthused and confident about their work. It is a creative process that generates fresh thinking and new strategies. With such a climate of collaboration, it comes as no surprise to find that it can also be enjoyable!

Practice points

- The purpose of supervision is to provide protection for clients and practitioners.
- Solution-focused supervision parallels the solution-focused process.
- Supervision 'coaxes the expertise' of the supervisee.
- Taking the 'one down' position opens up the learning space and encourages curiosity.
- Solution-focused supervision is respectful, collaborative and creative.
- The Reflecting Team model is a structured process that encourages good practice, builds team spirit and facilitates mutual learning.

8

Frequently Asked Questions
About SFT

In my experience as a trainer, there are always people at an introductory workshop who take to the approach with great enthusiasm. They champion it in their workplace. Others struggle with the radical nature of the model and are unclear how to integrate it with other interventions, while others claim to have been doing all of it already (with one or two extreme examples claiming to have been doing it even before de Shazer and his colleagues!) Some warm to the emphasis on solutions, but doubt that their clients will be either willing or able to co-operate. Using any new intervention with clients feels like a risk – it is usually easier to stay in your comfort zone and rely on the familiar, the tried and tested. To begin to use solution-focused language when one lacks fluency takes courage. It can be challenging when clients do not follow the script and, as a novice, you are searching for the next question. What gets practitioners through this phase is experiencing their clients engaging more positively with them and seeing them beginning to make real changes in their lives.

There are a number of questions that arise on a regular basis on courses and workshops and in this chapter I have attempted to answer them.

DOES THE METHOD IGNORE PEOPLE'S FEELINGS AND CONCENTRATE ON THEIR BEHAVIOUR?

Helping strategies differ in their understanding of the relationship between cognitions, emotions and behaviour. Some target the emotions primarily, others cognition and others behaviour. Others include all equally and regard therapies that do not do so as inherently defective. Many would argue that, to be effective, helping must address clients' needs holistically and be led by the clients' agendas and ways of experiencing the world. Failure to do so is likely to lead to them terminating the relationship.

Our feelings influence our thinking, our decisions and our actions. Expressing powerful feelings can be a catalyst for change. Solution-focused practitioners initiate and support clients in their expression of feelings – not because they believe that catharsis is in itself necessarily therapeutic, but because feelings are an integral part of our experience and that whole experience must be respected and validated.

Each client has different needs, with some needing to ventilate emotions more than others. In my view, it is helpful to retain as much manoeuvrability for the client and counsellor as possible. A pragmatic stance allows for greater choice so that clients do not feel that they must behave in a certain way for the process to work.

The focused nature of brief work precludes the wide-ranging emotional exploration possible in long-term work. It is probably true, that the amount of time spent directly exploring feelings in SFT is less than in some other models. De Shazer and Berg (1992), however, argue that helping the client to change the meaning of her experience automatically brings about a change in feelings regarding the problem. SFT tends to share the outlook of strategic counsellors (Kleckner, Frank, Bland, Amendt and Du Ree Bryant, 1992), who do not attempt to change people's feelings directly, but suggest that clients' feelings may catch up with changes in their attitudes or behaviour. Clients do not need to wait until they feel better before they begin to change aspects of their lives.

Fear of failure and ambivalence about change will affect people's willingness and ability to engage in the solution-focused process. When this is the case, motivational interview techniques that address this ambivalence (Prochaska, Di Clemente and Norcross, 1992) can supplement solution-focused interventions. When a client feels unsure or fearful about making changes, the counsellor will acknowledge her client's polarised feelings and adjust her approach accordingly.

At all stages of the process, the solution-focused approach validates and acknowledges clients' feelings. These feelings can emerge from pre-session change enquiries, exception-seeking questions, the miracle question, scaling exercises, goal negotiation and positive feedback to the client.

Solution-focused questioning can provoke strong expressions of feelings, not all of which are positive. The miracle question in particular, can access powerful feelings. In my own practice, clients have sometimes responded to the miracle question in tears – disclosing their despair about their lives, their rage against the world, their fear of the violence and abuse they are suffering, their sadness at a loss they have experienced. It is not all about positive thinking and happy feelings!

I would suggest that the co-operative, respectful, close, supportive climate generated in solution-focused interviews helps clients to feel safe to express their feelings.

IS THE SOLUTION-FOCUSED APPROACH EFFECTIVE OR IS IT POPULAR ONLY BECAUSE IT IS BRIEF AND THEREFORE ECONOMICAL?

There are many forms of brief counselling (see Chapter 1) and this question could apply to them all. Solution-focused work tends to be brief, but there is no reason per se for this to be the case. Some of its characteristics – such as staying close to the client's view of the problem, using what the client brings, setting attainable goals and refraining from a search for causes – are more likely to lead to the process being brief than long term.

However, some clients for one reason or another require long-term help and it is perfectly possible to use the approach with them.

We need to structure time so that it is an ally, not an enemy. Being aware that a first session may turn out to be the only one motivates the worker to make each session valuable and meaningful in its own right. Many practitioners work within severe time limitations and are constrained by targets. This can contribute to a distortion of the solution-focused approach, with goals being prematurely defined and strategies pushed forward by the worker in a futile attempt to resolve the problem within an agency timeframe.

IS SFT ONLY SUITABLE FOR CLIENTS WHO CAN IDENTIFY SPECIFIC ISSUES, NOT FOR THOSE WITH VAGUE, CHRONIC OR SEVERE MENTAL HEALTH PROBLEMS?
The implication behind this question is that SFT is useful in 'easy' cases, but not in more demanding ones. The reality is that the approach has been used in some of the most challenging settings imaginable, with clients who have chronic and complicated issues to address.

Very few clients come with clear, specific issues that they are motivated to address. Most come with a tangled web of conflicting emotions, thoughts, hopes and expectations. Many clients could well echo the sentiments of the serenity prayer: 'Give me the serenity to accept the things I cannot change, the courage to change the things I can and the wisdom to know the difference.' Knowing what to place in the 'change' box and what in the 'acceptance/serenity' box (M.F. O'Connell, 1997) is not always easy. Asking clients what they want to ensure they don't change can make it easier for them to look at the things they might want to change.

The solution-focused scepticism about assessment means that no category of problem or 'type' of client is, a priori, to be considered unsuitable. This reflects the constructionist view of how problems become attached to people and how this in turn affects the way in which professionals treat them. Mental health workers report that many clients with long-standing problems experience SFT as being quite different from other therapies they have received and this very novelty can help to break long-standing problem patterns. Such people will have little experience of being accepted as 'experts' in their own lives. Some may struggle to accept and trust their own strengths and qualities after a long period of dependency and learned helplessness. Others, however, will feel empowered and excited by the affirmation of their uniqueness.

The client may bring with them abilities such as:

- being open to describing the problem as solvable
- identifying what she wants to change
- feeling motivated to change
- recalling planned exceptions to the problem
- being willing to imagine a different future

- feeling committed to experimenting with change
- being able to own genuine compliments.

Without such strengths, the helping process may be slower and more uncertain in its outcome. However, it takes time for people to move from being a visitor or a complainant to being a customer. Even so, motivation can grow, insight can develop, action can emerge in small steps.

INVOLUNTARY OR MANDATED CLIENTS   Many clients are sent for help because someone else thinks that it is a good idea. The person often has power over them and demands to see change. The clients may be feeling resentful, angry, confused and hostile. They may be reluctant to own an agenda and unwilling to answer questions. They may not trust the confidentiality of the relationship and so be on their guard, not wanting to give anything away. They may see the counsellor as being on the side of authority. In such circumstances, the counsellor will have to earn the client's trust. Turnell and Edwards (1999: 30) offer useful guidelines for working with clients who want to keep professionals at a distance. Their research concerned families under investigation by social workers for suspected child abuse. I have adapted some of their practice principles to meet a range of situations:

- co-operate with the person, not the problem behaviour
- respect service recipients as people with whom it is worth doing business
- recognise that co-operation is possible, even if, ultimately, professional intervention is required
- recognise that all clients are doing some things that are helpful and constructive
- maintain a focus on positive goals
- learn what the service recipient wants
- always search for detail
- don't confuse details with judgments
- focus on creating small change
- offer choices
- treat the interview as a forum for change
- treat these principles as aspirations, not assumptions.

Keeping to these practice principles is likely to lead to more co-operation from clients than would otherwise be the case. Most solution-focused counsellors report that its 'light touch' helps to gain and sustain the engagement of the reluctant client as long as she is fully consulted about the agenda. Once clients sense that we are 'on their side', in the sense that we want them to achieve their life goals (providing they are compatible with the rights of others), and that we are willing to work with them in ways that fit their context, it is striking how low the dropout rate is.

EXAMPLE

Counsellor: So what's brought you here today?

Client: My boss has been complaining about me. He says that if I don't change after coming here, then I'm going to lose my job.

Counsellor: How do you feel about that?

Client: I feel really angry. Why should I be the one who comes for counselling? I feel that I'm being blamed for the whole thing and I don't think that's fair.

Counsellor: You feel that you've been unfairly blamed and don't see why you should be the one to change.

Client: That's right.

Counsellor: What would need to happen do you think before they stopped blaming you?

Client: I don't know.

[Silence]

Counsellor: You're not sure what they want from you.

Client: No.

Counsellor: What would they say if you asked them?

Client: That I don't let my personal problems interfere with my work, I suppose.

Counsellor: If you think that's how they see it, what would you notice that was different at work if they were interfering less?

Client: I wouldn't be off sick so often. I'd be enjoying my work again. At the moment I hate going in, I just don't want to be there.

Counsellor: What would be different for you if you were enjoying it just a bit better?

Client: I'd be out and about more and not stuck in the office all the time. That's the part of the job I like best, visiting the customers. I've known some of them for years. But they've taken me off that, until I sort my problems out.

Counsellor: What do you need to do to get that part of the job back?

Client: I need to prove that I'm more reliable.

Counsellor: How could you do that?

Client: By getting in on time, not being off sick. Coming back after lunch. Getting my paperwork up to date.

Counsellor: Does any of that happen at the moment?

Client: It's been a bit of a bad patch recently. I'm usually very healthy, but it's just been one thing after the other.

Counsellor: You've been having a tough time. What do you think would be the first sign to your boss that you've started to be more reliable again?

Client: Being at my desk for 8.30 I suppose.

Counsellor: Is that something you want to do?

Client: Yes.

Counsellor: What would need to happen for that to happen?

Client: I used to always be the first in the place, I was dead keen. I'd need to tell myself that I had to do it if I wanted to get out of this mess.

Counsellor: How long will it be before you feel like that do you think?

Client: I feel like it now. It's just doing it.

In the first place, it is important for the counsellor to validate the client's perception of the situation, otherwise she will be seen by the client as a tool of the commissioning agency. This does not mean that one agrees with the client's version, but it is an acknowledgement of the client's feelings and opinions. Second, it is essential to keep as close as possible to the client's stated agenda, which may differ from that of the referral source. This helps to eliminate the 'Yes, but ...' exchanges that result when the client argues against any change in the status quo while the counsellor proposes solutions. In effective solution-focused interviews, there will be a symmetry between the client and the counsellor, with the balance of talking being slightly on the side of the client. Third, the counsellor may need to seek the collaboration of the referring agency in negotiating goals for the client and supporting him in working towards them.

'ABSENT CLIENTS'   Many clients feel that their prospects of change are blighted by a key person in the system who refuses to acknowledge the problem or co-operate in solving it. This could be a partner who buries his or her head in the sand by denying or trivialising the problem, a colleague who has power over the client in the workplace, or a non-cooperative family member. They are not customers for change; they refuse to accept the client's description of the problem or take responsibility for the perceived consequences of their actions on others. Despite the frustrations and hopelessness such a situation generates, the solution-focused questions in Figure 8.1 can be helpful.

Hudson and O'Hanlon (1991) suggest that, on occasion, it is possible to bring the absent party into the counselling if they are reassured that they will not be the focus of blame and if they can be convinced that the counsellor really wants to hear their side of the story.

IS THERE A DANGER THAT SFT ONLY ADDRESSES SYMPTOMS AND DOES NOT DEAL WITH THE UNDERLYING ISSUES THAT MAY THEREFORE RE-EMERGE? Durrant (1997), focusing on the power of language in problem construction, states that there are only underlying issues if you talk about them in that way. The solution-focused conversation does allow for clients to offer explanations, make connections and identify past influences and events, but the solution-focused counsellor does not believe that current difficulties are resolved by identifying 'underlying issues'. In many respects, the distinction between symptoms and underlying issues is unhelpful. Real and lasting personal change can begin anywhere – there is no one route to change. Achieving resolution of a current problem can give a very different perspective on the past. Re-authoring (White, 1995) the past can enable the future to become a different story and constructing the future can influence the present (the miracle question). It should not be an automatic assumption that clients need to undertake the 'insight' route to change. Experience suggests that the more options there are the better, as long as there are not enough of them to confuse everyone. Helping can get bogged down when there is a belief, from either side, that certain things must happen, perhaps even in a certain order, if genuine progress is to be made. It is worth remembering at this point that solution-focused conversations can become 'deep' quite quickly – clients will often express surprise at how quickly they accessed powerful feelings and ideas.

- Who wants change the most? What would be the benefits of change for everyone concerned?
- Who has the ability to deliver change?
- Where does the power lie and could its distribution be changed?
- Is there a more helpful way of reading the situation?
- What would constitute a reasonable improvement, even if the basic situation remained unaltered?
- What does the client have the power to change?
- What difference would it make if the client was able to make those changes?
- How can the client stop the situation deteriorating?
- What might be the short- and long-term options?
- What would it mean for the client if she chose to accept some aspects of the situation?
- What could the client do that was different from what she usually does?
- Is the client trying too hard to change the situation?
- Would it be more helpful to stop any direct action for the time being?
- Could the client stop the 'failed solutions' he has used?
- Who/what helps her to cope with this situation?
- How could she do more of what helps him to cope?
- Is she underestimating her power and overestimating the power of the other?
- How would she know this was happening?
- Have there been any times when he managed the situation a little better?
- Is there any time when the other person acts in the way she wants, even for a few moments? If so, how did she do that?
- What difference did that make for the client?
- On a scale of zero to ten, where would she rate this problem today?
- What would need to happen for her to move up one point on the scale?
- How long does she think it will take before she sees some progress up the scale?
- Imagine the other person does not change at all, but a miracle happens for the client, what would be the signs for her that a miracle had happened?
- What does the client like about the way she is handling this very difficult situation?
- What will be the first signs for the client that the situation is showing some improvement?
- Is this as bad as it gets or is it likely to get worse?
- If so, how long would she want/be able to put up with it?
- When would she know that she had reached her limit?

Figure 8.1   *Solution-focused questions when the 'client is absent'*

No form of counselling offers a lifetime guarantee that the client will be free of problems. Counsellors whose training taught them that they must assess the client's history carefully before entering into a contract, are likely to feel uneasy with a model that does not see the past as a necessary starting point. It is indisputable that some clients do find it helpful to link their current problems with, for example, patterns in their families of origin. It is not a question of denying that we all can learn from our personal and collective past, but, rather, that we can come to that learning from many different angles and it may come more as an ending than a beginning. Sometimes we need to get to a new vantage point before we can make sense of the past.

EXAMPLE

Counsellor: From what you've both told me, it sounds as if there was not much love or affection demonstrated in Jak's family when he was small, but more in yours, Jean.

Jak: We're agreed on that. It's left me having difficulties showing affection to anyone. I'd like to be more demonstrative with the kids and with Jean, but it isn't easy – my dad never showed any affection to me.

Jean: You're not like your dad, though, Jak. He was more interested in things outside the home. He was just like a lot of dads at that time.

Counsellor: How do you feel you're different from your dad, Jak?

Jak: I'm a lot more involved with the kids. If I have to go away on work, I always speak to them on the phone every day. When I am at home, we do a lot more things as a family. I know the things they're into … I've seen how Jean is always hugging and cuddling the kids. I'd like to do that more often, but I find I hold back. Having said that, I'm better than I used to be – now I sometimes cuddle them when we're sitting watching television. I couldn't do that a couple of years ago.

Counsellor: So it's not come as naturally to you as it did for Jean. Have you noticed, Jean, how much he has been trying?

Jean: He's getting there. He's even getting round to kissing me when he comes and goes – that's progress!

Counsellor: Do you think, Jak, that being more affectionate towards Jean and showing more affection to the kids go together or do you see them as separate?

Jak: I never saw my mum and dad kiss, never. It was a shock when I went to Jean's house and saw her parents with their arms round each other. I think it's nice for children to see their parents love each other. I want my family life to be much warmer than mine was.

(Continued)

> (*Continued*)
>
> *Counsellor:*   What's it like now when you cuddle the kids sometimes and give Jean a kiss when you come in or go out?
> *Jak:*   I like it, it's more like a real family.
> *Counsellor:*   Do you think that you will keep this up and even get better at it over the next few months?
> *Jak:*   I'd like to be more spontaneous about it – at the moment it feels forced and awkward.
> *Counsellor:*   So, to begin with, you have to think about it first then do it, but you'd like to get to the stage when you do it without thinking or planning it. It just happens.
> *Jak:*   Yes.

Is SFT NAÏVE IN THAT IT TAKES THE STORIES CLIENTS PRESENT AT FACE VALUE?

As far as possible, the solution-focused practitioner works with whatever the client brings. There is no reading between the lines to unearth the 'real' problem. What is important is creating safe, therapeutic time and space so that the client can express what she wants in the way that she wants. If this happens, the client will feel able to disclose what she feels is important. We realise how painful and difficult it is for clients to reveal aspects of themselves about which they feel ashamed or guilty or confused. We do not need to interpret this as denial, rationalisation or resistance, but, rather, as the client choosing the level of co-operation she feels is appropriate at the time. Issues not initially disclosed – for example, abuse or discrimination – often emerge as the client begins to address the chosen agenda. A growing sense of self-empowerment, supported by the respect and affirmation shown to her can make it easier for the client to talk about 'the shadow side'. For some practitioners untrained in the solution-focused approach, the thought of not probing and formulating an understanding of the client's past would provoke anxiety and a fear of missing the 'real' issue. It is a big jump for them to trust the client to talk about what she needs to talk about (see Figure 8.2 for questions that help evaluate progress and offer opportunities for the client to mention other things that they may have felt wary of disclosing at first).

> - Are you finding this helpful?
> - Is this what you wanted to talk about?
> - Is there anything else you want to tell me about?
> - Is there anything you feel that it is important for me to know?
> - Do you think I know enough in order to help?

Figure 8.2   *Evaluating progress*

IS SOLUTION-FOCUSED THERAPY AN ETHICAL WAY OF WORKING?
It is important that counsellors are accountable to a supervisor and a professional organisation. They need to subscribe to a code of practice and a transparent complaints procedure. Practitioners need to practice the core values and conditions of person-centred work and be aware of the impact that their own values have. Otherwise, they will, at best, employ solution-focused formulae without heart or spirit and, at worst, undermine the client's autonomy.

While there are always tensions and conflicts about general ethical principles, it is important for solution-focused counsellors to have the knowledge and expertise to make ethical and professional decisions based on them. Bond (1993) cites five key principles:

- autonomy – respect for the client's right to be self-governing
- beneficence – a commitment to promoting the client's well-being
- non-maleficence – a commitment to avoiding harm to the client
- justice – the fair and impartial treatment of all clients and provision of adequate services
- fidelity – honouring the trust placed in the practitioner.

Strategic family therapy and the MRI model (close relatives of SFT) have both been criticised in the past as being manipulative and devious. Clients were, for example, given paradoxical tasks, such as the prescription of their symptoms or being warned against getting better too soon.

In SFT there is less reliance on giving clients unusual or 'tricky' assignments and more emphasis on clients devising their own tasks. Practitioners choose 'to give their power away' by demystifying the therapeutic process and explaining to clients, in either pre-sessional literature or the sessions themselves, exactly what is entailed so that clients can give their informed consent.

IS SFT SUITABLE FOR CROSS-CULTURAL WORK?
De Shazer does not address the cross-cultural dimension of SFT, although it is a central issue in Western societies with multicultural communities. Issues around difference and anti-oppressive practice are bitterly contested. The value-free neutral position is not available.

Many solution-focused practitioners see the 'one down' position advocated by the model to be particularly relevant in this regard. Taking this position allows the practitioner to become a learner and 'guest' in the client's culture. This attitude confers a respectful validation on the clients' perceptions and values, including their social context, sexuality and stage of racial identity development. White (2003: 90) finds it a relief to use a model that allows him to put the client in the expert position, particularly in cross-cultural work, 'where the degree of my ignorance is greater than usual.' This openness to other cultures is a necessity when working in a multicultural, multifaith institution such as a school (Ratner, 2003). The emphasis on client strengths and competence ensures that the client's cultural resources are routinely viewed as part of the solution, while there is an awareness that cultural values and practices may be a major influence in configuring the pace and type of change. Jointly constructed descriptions of the client's experience also encourage a respect for difference and reduce the impact of the practitioner's values.

Data from a small sample of clients at the Brief Family Therapy Centre in Milwaukee (De Jong and Hopwood, 1996) suggest that different racial groups show little difference in outcome and that client–counsellor racial mix is not related to the outcomes of SFT.

DOES THE EMPHASIS ON GOALS AND SOLUTIONS MEAN THAT THE MODEL PARTICULARLY APPEALS TO MALE COUNSELLORS AND CLIENTS?

Some of the leading SFT practitioners are women – among them Weiner-Davis, Lipchik, Hudson, Metcalf, Berg and Dolan. Practitioners have used the model extensively with female clients who were survivors of child abuse (Dolan, 1998), had suffered sexual trauma (Darmody, 2003) and violence, or were recovering from eating disorders (Jacob, 2001). Lethem (1994: 33) argues that the model 'has the capacity to validate the experiences of women, acknowledge the contribution of social injustice to many of their difficulties and offer them opportunities to utilise strengths they may have overlooked in resolving problems and dilemmas.'

De Jong and Hopwood (1996), in a small study that they warn needs to be read with caution, assert that women and men have equally positive outcomes, whether the counsellors using the model were men or women. Bailey-Martiniere (1993) argues that the model validates and communicates respect to women by:

- listening without pathologising or interpreting her problem as a symptom of an underlying issue located in the past
- viewing her as an expert with strengths and resources
- using the miracle question to establish goals, rather than the ideas and biases of the counsellor about what a woman should or should not do
- reframing problems as ordinary life experiences, liberating her from guilt and stereotypes such as victim and non-coper
- equipping her with tools for change
- avoiding endless emotional unburdening or analysis that can reinforce helplessness and depression
- discouraging passivity, fatalism and self-defeating talk
- helping women to articulate their own hopes and empowering them to act to create their own solutions.

These powerful qualities make the model eminently suitable for women clients and counsellors. Lethem (1994: 31) claims that the model respects both 'the tears and the desire for action', while Dolan (1998: 9), who draws heavily on solution-focused ideas for her many creative exercises for women recovering from the effects of abuse, believes that the solution-focused 'posture of respect, pragmatism and hopefulness is uniquely suited to people who have survived physical, emotional and sexual abuse and other traumas.'

Practice points

- Solution-focused language can feel like a foreign language at first. It takes time to become fluent.
- In cross-cultural work, the practitioner is a curious and respectful guest in the client's culture.
- Always validate and acknowledge clients' feelings.
- It can be helpful to check with clients what they don't want to change.
- Concentrate on the person, not the problem behaviour.
- Solution-focused work should be open and jointly owned by worker and client.

9

An Integrative Solution-focused Approach

Solution-focused thinking has influenced a wide range of non-therapist practitioners. Their varied skills include advocacy, coaching, mentoring, teaching, running groups, giving advice and information, mediation, offering healthcare and practical assistance with accommodation and employment issues. Some of these services require the worker to offer direction or guidance. In theory this seems inconsistent with solution-focused principles, but in practice many people in the field handle this tension without undue angst. Non-therapists tend to be more pragmatic and less purist than some therapists. This absence of ideological baggage enables them to 'use what works and leave what doesn't' in order to meet the needs of their clients. Their integrative practice means that they look for ways to adapt the classic solution-focused interventions to the specific context of their agency.

In Chapter 2 I briefly referred to the different stages through which followers of new theories or systems of belief pass as they seek to propagate their ideas. According to Schwartz (1955), a defensiveness, coupled with an evangelical spirit, characterise the earlier stages. Tensions between different wings develop as the modernisers begin to modify the orthodox tradition in order to assimilate other progressive schools of thought. There are similar tensions within the solution-focused movement between practitioners who advocate using only solution-focused methods and others who are more open to integrating with other therapeutic interventions. This chapter examines how the solution-focused approach can usefully incorporate ideas and practices from other models that are based on different assumptions and aims and how other therapeutic models could gain from integrating solution-focused elements. This chapter refers specifically to therapy.

It is generally accepted that, while at the level of theory there are incompatible differences between different schools of therapy, in practice therapists are increasingly drawing on a range of techniques without subscribing to the theory behind them. This technical eclecticism (Lazarus, 1981) is atheoretical and pragmatic. It is consistent with SFT's emphasis on shedding unnecessary ideology and focusing on what works for the client. SFT advocates doing something different when therapy is 'stuck' and this includes borrowing techniques from other approaches.

The movement towards greater consensus between and convergence of different therapeutic approaches is based on the following evidence:

- The theoretical orientation of the therapist is unimportant to clients, at least in comparison to the personality of the therapist, her experience or the quality of the therapeutic relationship (Brown and Lent, 1992).
- Therapists do not, in practice, conform to the 'purist' theoretical models to which they subscribe (Schapp, Bennun, Schindler and Hoogduin, 1993).
- In general terms, there is equality of outcome for different approaches (research summarised in Garfield and Bergin, 1994). No one model can claim superiority. Duncan (1992) criticises models that claim universal application and effectiveness. He suggests that the experience of practitioners is that nothing *always* works and that no one model is sufficient to address the complexity of the human condition or the uniqueness of individuals.
- Lambert (1986) identified that as much as 30 per cent of outcome variance is related to common factors. He found that techniques were no more powerful than the placebo effect, both of which account for approximately 15 per cent of the positive outcome variance.
- The emergence of brief therapy as the norm for practice has helped to identify a set of characteristics common to most time-limited models and more significant than any differences between them. These characteristics are:

  – accepting people as competent
  – forming the therapeutic alliance as quickly as possible
  – giving the client credit for progress and success
  – focusing on clear, specific, attainable goals
  – projection of the therapist as competent, hopeful and confident
  – the work having a clear focus
  – accepting the client's view of the problem
  – avoiding a power struggle with the client.

Taking an inclusive integrative position, allows us to look at other ways of working to explore the common ground in terms of values, styles of relationships, use of language and techniques. Solution-focused practice gives, gets and borrows from other approaches. In terms of values and relationships, SFT has much common ground with person-centred therapy.

Person-centred therapy

At first sight, there appears to be little common ground between SFT and person-centred therapy. Some person-centred practitioners regard any practitioner-led interventions, such as those used in SFT, as fundamentally incompatible with the person-centred approach. Merry (1990), for example, argues that therapist-initiated interventions constitute a breach of the 'here and now' quality of the counsellor–client encounter. This interference with the client's natural processes – for example, staying with painful experiences – he sees as arising from the insecurity and anxiety of the counsellor under pressure to produce results and feel helpful. In Merry's (1990: 18) opinion this means that, 'the therapist's expertise, technique and power take precedence over the client's personal power.'

Wilkins (1993) takes a more liberal line, distinguishing between person-centred *therapy*, which he sees as a therapeutic model with its own particular methodology, and a person-centred approach, which uses interventions congruent with person-centred core values, such as respect for the autonomy of the client. In my view, SFT meets this latter criterion because it enters into the client's frame of reference, disowns the role of expert, affirms and respects the client's experiences, builds on the client's essential healthiness, keeps close to the client's goals and trusts the client to know how to overcome his problems and when to end the work. Figure 9.1 illustrates how using the solution-focused approach with people suffering from mental illness affirms core person-centred values.

Values	SFT
Respect	Allowing clients time to explore, air their views. Collaborate and create possibilities.
Recognising people as experts in their experiences	As therapists, we may have expert knowledge and skills, but recognise the client's expertise in experience. The therapist accepts that they can learn from the client.
People are more than an illness	The diagnosis is not a focus – the consequences of the experience are what impact people's lives. The client is seen as a survivor or victor rather than a victim. The client has strengths.
Valued for more than your financial worth	Everyone is already doing something of value some of the time. We all have something to contribute. The client is seen as resourceful.
Inclusion	The client is central to the intervention, and defines where they want to be. The therapist helps to identify the direction of goals determined by the client. The client is encouraged to generate solutions, not be problem solved. Success is more likely as we enter the client's frame of reference and utilise solution patterns that already exist.
Seen as individuals	The solution-focused framework provides a process that is flexible in terms of providing individually tailored interventions that are different for each client. People's uniqueness is celebrated.

Capable of reason	The client helps define and map out where they want to be. The client is encouraged to take positive risks. The client is the best judge – knows when he has arrived at where he wants to be.
Aspirations	Fundamental belief in change, which is constant and inevitable. People are allowed a preferred future.
Beliefs	There is no failure, just different ways of doing things. If things don't have the desired outcome, the therapist and client accept that they may need to do things differently. Resistance is the client's unique way of cooperating. People's experiences are seen as valid and understandable. The intervention is about facilitating change, rather than defining problems and weaknesses.
Flexibility	Meetings are arranged in line with the client's pace of change. A common language is used, rather than professional jargon.
Risk management	Clients are actively involved in risk management strategies. Coping strategies are shared and collaborative.
Opportunity	Positive images of the future are constructed and attained in small steps. The therapist encourages the client to use opportunities to move towards their goals. The opportunity to make small changes, affecting wider systems, is created.

Figure 9.1 *Solution-focused values (Dodd, 2003)*

Payne (1993) sees the 'technique' of externalisation (see Chapter 5), which narrative and solution-focused therapy use, as being compatible with Rogerian values. In particular, he lists the areas of common ground as being:

- a belief that clients always have the potential for self-derived growth and change
- a rejection of 'unconscious' explanations and processes as unknowable and of limited usefulness
- a belief that the central aim is to promote the empowerment of the client
- a range of positive, human, optimistic perspectives
- a conviction that clients have the ability to reorganise 'interiorised' experience as a route to overcoming problems.

SFT provides certain structures – such as the miracle question, scaling and exception seeking – that enable clients to explore their own feelings, thoughts and ideas about their lives. Every form of therapy, including person-centred, sets boundaries for the therapeutic encounter and seeks to influence the client. It is not possible to avoid influencing the client – it would be a strange use of resources if the client was not influenced by what happened in therapy. However, influencing, while respecting client autonomy, is different from prescribing for the client what the practitioner considers to be the way forward. I think, therefore, that it can be argued that SFT has a legitimate claim to consider itself to be person-centred.

The TFA model

A central theme of this book has been the importance of language and the need to build collaborative relationships with clients. Hutchins' (1989) TFA model is a useful integrating tool for the solution-focused practitioner to use to remind herself of the importance of language and the need to 'live in the client's linguistic world.'

He suggests that practitioners need to be aware of both their clients' and their own dominant ways of experiencing the world. He identifies these modes as thinking, feeling and acting, hence TFA. Practitioners become aware of their clients' orientation by paying careful attention to how they talk about their problems. Although we are a mixture of all three elements, we are likely to have a bias towards one or another. Hutchins suggests that, in order to form a working alliance, practitioners should match the client's language, so that if the person speaks in feeling-orientated terms, the practitioner responds, at least initially, in kind. Matching modes of communication requires the practitioner to adapt to meet the client 'where he is' – a principle congruent with the SFT custom of 'joining with' and learning from the client. If, for example, the practitioner knew that she had a strong action orientation and that the client had a strong feeling orientation, this would caution her against rushing towards solutions, instead taking time to validate and explore the client's feelings. If, however, the practitioner is predominantly a 'thinker' and the client a 'doer', she will need to ensure that her need for thinking time does not unduly delay the client from acting.

Most competent practitioners intuitively match their clients' language. This framework helps them to do it in a more systematic and planned way. It encourages a productive start and so diffuses potential tensions and conflicts. The most effective practitioners will be those who adapt to a wide range of clients. Hutchins (1989) also advocates that practitioners should, at least initially, build on the client's TFA strengths – an idea that clearly resonates with SFT. It is also important to be responsive to the client's dominant modes in order to construct solutions that 'fit' the client.

Increased self-awareness about his TFA profile can enable the practitioner to adapt the model to his personality rather than the other way round. In my view, when practitioners do not feel congruent with the model, it causes significant stress and negatively impacts the therapeutic relationship.

The Cycle of Change model

Another model that many solution-focused practitioners – particularly in the substance misuse field – find useful is the Cycle of Change model (Prochaska, Di Clemente and Norcross, 1992). The Cycle of Change model, although differing significantly from SFT in terms of theoretical assumptions, is a useful tool for developing the solution-focused practitioner's thinking about the client's current readiness for change.

SFT uses the descriptions of visitor, complainant and customer to describe the 'constructed positions' of clients in relation to change. The five-stage cycle of change model describes a process that people may go through as they attempt to change their behaviour. Progress is not linear. Individuals may revisit previous stages or remain stuck in one stage for a long time. The model takes into account that people usually have some form of problem relapse. The five stages are as follows:

1   *Pre-contemplation* At this stage a person is a reluctant or involuntary client with little or no authentic motivation. The person may feel overwhelmed by the problem and unable to take the first step in what seems to them to be a long and painful journey.

2   *Contemplation* A contemplator wants to want to change, but does not feel ready to do so and will procrastinate. Previous attempts to change have not been sustained. She may need to see those 'failures' as temporary exceptions to the problem.

3   *Preparation* The client has begun to plan seriously how to overcome the problem by making initial decisions and engaging others to offer support.

4   *Action* The person has taken steps to make the desired changes and begun to implement a plan.

5   *Maintenance* In this stage, the client has some success in maintaining the problem-free behaviour, but may also have relapses and return to earlier phases of the cycle. Some people break out of the cycle altogether and no longer consider themselves to have the problem; others feel that they are on maintenance guard for a long time or even for the rest of their lives.

The Cycle of Change model and SFT

A working knowledge of the cycle of change can help the solution-focused practitioner to be aware of how to engage with the client appropriately.

1   *Pre-contemplation* Some of the strategies described in Chapter 8 for use with reluctant clients or 'visitors' (de Shazer, 1988) are relevant at this stage. These include accepting the client's current ambivalence, not trying to argue for change, helping the client to formulate a goal, imagining with the client circumstances in which he might want to change.

2   *Contemplation* This is similar to the 'complainant' (de Shazer, 1988) position in which the client identifies a problem or goal, but feels ambivalent or helpless when it comes to tackling it. Here the counsellor may seek to shift the focus from the problem and emphasise instead competence, exceptions and the future, as revealed by the miracle question. The client may not be ready for 'doing' tasks but may be willing to engage in 'noticing' tasks.

3   *Preparation* At this point, the client is willing to think about possible solutions and discuss 'what would need to happen for that to happen'. He may be willing to engage in 'experiments'. Setting clear, realistic and attainable goals and identifying both personal and environmental resources are important at this stage.

4   *Action* The client is a 'customer for change' (de Shazer, 1988). The counsellor reinforces constructive change and encourages the client to keep doing what is helpful.

5   *Maintenance* The solution-focused counsellor will have discussed maintenance strategies with the client and warned of the possibility of relapses. A contingency plan will have been agreed. The worker may use scaling to highlight how the client stopped the situation deteriorating – 'If you were at one, how did you avoid it becoming zero?' He will continue to look for exceptions and help the client to learn from setbacks. He will help the client to construe what has happened in ways that do not trap her in the problem or disempower her in the face of failure. He may wish to explore with the client when and how she could discard her 'problem' identity – for example, as an alcoholic, anorexic or survivor of abuse.

As well as discovering links with other approaches that strengthen the values base and enhance the quality of the therapeutic alliance, there is a rich array of techniques in other approaches that can be integrated into the solution-focused frame. In order to demonstrate this, the following section describes how techniques borrowed from cognitive-behavioural therapy (CBT) can become solution-focused interventions.

SFT and CBT

Cognitive-behavioural therapy (CBT) highlights how certain thinking patterns lead to a distorted picture of what is going on in our lives, how 'we do not see things as they are, but as we are' (Anaïs Nin). Clients who sabotage themselves by their negative and self-defeating outlook need to target the thinking that disempowers them. This process can be enhanced by merging solution-focused and CB skills.

Replacing destructive beliefs

When clients' beliefs about themselves and their situation causes them problems, the aim is to help them to change their thinking and substitute non-problematic beliefs. In CBT, the counsellor first explores the old belief with the client, inviting him to cite the evidence for it (there is bound to be some). This parallels the acknowledgment and validation of the client's concerns in SFT. Then the client is asked to rate on a scale of 0 to 100 how strongly they hold this belief (with 100 being the strongest). The CBT practitioner does not interfere with the client's judgement (this is similar to the solution-focused principle of 'getting out of the client's way.')

They next negotiate a modified version of the belief – one that is non-problematic for the client. Having formulated this new belief, the client is invited to look for evidence to strengthen this new belief and also for evidence that will undermine and weaken the original belief. In solution-focused terms, this is a 'search for exceptions'. As clients reflect on their findings, they are invited to rate the strength of each belief. When the modified belief is stronger than the problematic belief, the client will have developed the required mental strength to overcome the problem.

This use of scaling in CBT can be strengthened by the scaling questions used in SFT. SFT scaling will help clients to identify 'the difference that made the difference.' It will help to identify the small steps that the clients took to move up or down the scale. The questions used in solution-focused exception seeking will also be useful. These questions can help to reinforce and expand the client's new learning.

Constructing explanations

One way in which we create problems for ourselves is by adopting explanations for or interpretations of our experiences that make the situation worse. Our use of language creates our realities. Given a choice, it is preferable to read a situation in a way that opens up solutions, not reinforces a problem. Some mental habits that can expand the problem include:

- discounting positive and/or exaggerating negative information
- negative generalising from a specific situation
- over- or under-owning responsibility
- reasoning emotionally.

The solution-focused approach can help to explore these mental habits by:

- reflecting back 'evidence' as the client's subjective perception or feeling
- inviting clients to consider alternative explanations and, if they are willing, offer another perspective.

Encourage clients to be aware of their use of language and to consider whether changing the language they use might help them to see things differently. In general terms, rigid, closed thinking contributes to problems and more flexible, open ways of thinking lead to more solutions.

Journal of Solutions
In CBT, clients are routinely asked to keep a diary of their thinking. A solution-focused version of this is for clients to keep a journal of times when they would have expected to be angry/depressed/anxious, but managed to avoid this. In their journal they may reflect on questions such as the following.

- What was I thinking about at that time?
- What self-talk did I use?
- Who or what helped?
- What do I conclude from this?

Automatic thoughts
We all experience having unwelcome, uninvited thoughts. They can be positive or negative, happy or unhappy or a mix of both. Negative thoughts are likely to heighten anxious or unhappy moods. We know that the more we think about a problem in an unhelpful way, the bigger it gets. Thinking becomes a form of self-indoctrination, leading to self-fulfilling prophecies.

In order to overcome negative thoughts, the client needs to become aware that he or she is going into these 'trances' and learn how to combat them. A solution-focused perspective invites the client to remember times when they might have begun to go into 'negative trance', but somehow managed to resist it. We would ask the client how she managed to do that and how she could do it again. We may help the client to prepare an alternative sequence of thinking to break the trance. Figuratively speaking, for example, we all have a stock of videos in our head and we can choose to play one to combat the negative thoughts. The video will be of an enjoyable event that reminds us of positive experiences.

Integrating experiential techniques from other models

Experiential exercises
These exercises are practitioner-facilitated activities that provide the client with an immediate awareness-raising experience. There is a wide

range of activities, including role playing, psychodrama, fantasy and drawing. It is advisable to be trained in these techniques before using them with clients.

Many therapies are overly reliant on the left side of the brain, which controls rationality, analysis and verbal fluency, but, as Washburn (1994) points out, this mirroring of academia disenfranchises many people who operate in a predominantly right-sided (holistic, spatially orientated, non-verbal, artistic, intuitive) way and who may have a history of failure resulting from poor performance in left-sided tasks. Washburn (1994: 52) argues that brief solution-orientated therapy, 'with its focus on successes, tasks, concrete goals and assessment, is less likely to alienate the person with right brain dominance.' He sees SFT as having advantages for such people because its emphasis on concreteness rather than abstraction, action instead of insight appeals to people whose right side of the brain is dominant. This may also mean that it is more user-friendly for children and people with learning or speech difficulties. The benefit for the practitioner of including non-verbal, experiential activities is that they facilitate access to people's emotional lives and act as a counterbalance to the inherent intellectualism of verbal approaches. Experiential activities can also ensure that the present is experienced as therapeutic and not merely an exchange of information about past events or future goals. Another advantage of integrating experiential activities with SFT is that they often access feelings, ideas and memories that may not be reached by standard questions.

DRAMA

Bischof (1993) encourages clients to dramatise situations in which they experienced an exception to their problem, then discuss what it was that made the difference. He works in a similar way with the miracle question. He invites clients to imagine waking up after the miracle has happened and act out some of the ensuing scenes, with the therapist taking the parts of family members, friends or colleagues. If others have accompanied the client to therapy, the client sculpts the scene, positioning them according to how he envisages them after the miracle. If the client is reluctant to act out the scene, an alternative for the client is to place coins or other objects on a table and place them where they would be before and after the miracle and explore her feelings and thoughts during the exercise.

Clients may also dramatise the zero to ten scale by placing numbered cards on the floor like stepping stones. The client places himself in line according to where he thinks he is today, moves to where he would like to get to, then explores what he would need to do to move up one point on the scale. The practitioner may ask the client how he feels and what he is thinking as the client stands at different points on the scale. Clients who have taken part in this exercise report that the physical act of taking up a position increases ownership and motivation.

Exercises from other experiential therapies can be given a solution-focused orientation. For example, the empty chair sometimes used in Gestalt to represent an absent person can be given a solution-orientated twist. In this, the practitioner suggests that the client construct an imaginary dialogue with the absent person, concentrating on competences, strengths, compliments, exceptions, goals and strategies. This technique requires considerable skill, so it is not recommended to inexperienced practitioners as it can be a powerful emotional experience for the client.

DRAWING

Experiential activities, such as drawing or sculpting, can bypass inhibitions and generate ideas and feelings about solutions otherwise beyond the client's awareness and capacity for verbal expression. Clients may be invited to draw scales, miracle scenarios or scenes portraying exceptions to the problem. Sharing these can facilitate learning. I have also experimented with encouraging clients to draw strip cartoons of miracles, exceptions, strengths and goals, and have been amazed at how inventive people can be. Collar (2004) reports on the success of getting a group of children to make a model of problem island. This led to so much discussion that they never quite got around to building solution island!

THERAPEUTIC LETTER WRITING

Many approaches advocate writing therapeutic letters to clients and inviting clients to compose letters in which they discharge their thoughts and feelings. These letters are not intended to be sent. Other approaches encourage clients to keep diaries or journals. Some solution-focused practitioners write to their clients after each session to summarise the content of the feedback and reinforce the client's constructive actions. Sometimes clients request this, as they often cannot remember clearly enough the feedback given at the end of the session.

As part of their 'homework' the practitioner asks clients to keep a record of occasions when they would have expected to have experienced the problem but did not, or times when something constructive happened that they would like to see continue. This could include observations of other people's behaviour or detailed accounts of particular solution incidents. They may use a diary to keep note of their predictions or record their day-to-day use of scaling. Anything that they do, say, think or feel and consider to be helpful is recorded to be given as feedback in the next session. The record becomes a book of solutions.

Nunnally and Lipchik (1989) describe using letters to clients as reminders of their tasks; as a supplement when something important was missed in the end of the session message; and for inviting clarification of goals following a confusing session. Writing can itself be a therapeutic release that, in turn, alters the problem situations. Writing can be a form of 'doing something different'. It can be helpful for both client and counsellor to write about their experience at the end of a course of therapy. The following is a brief account written by a client at the end of therapy. He had been suffering from anxiety and panic attacks that affected his work performance, driving and home life.

> I decided to seek help because I had not been able to resolve the situation myself after three years' struggling. I had resisted getting help because I felt I could handle it alone – and if I wasn't able to handle it then I was worried I would be getting ill. Following a visit to my GP I began to take Paroxetene. While the medication has not been the whole answer, it has allowed me the space to put activities in place of anxieties.
>
> The first thing that helped was realising that what I called 'symptoms' should more accurately be called 'signals'. These signals were signs sent to my body by my mind to tell me that my mind was having some difficulty in handling something, but mostly it was having difficulty handling the signals! So I needed to develop means to disregard the signals.
>
> I developed a number of techniques for handling the immediate situation:
>
> - ignore the feeling
> - think of something else
> - blank out my mind
> - picture something in my mind
> - imagine a protective 'ring' around me of the car
> - breathe slowly and feel my whole lungs fill, then slowly exhale
> - stabilise my breathing to a steady rhythm.
>
> While none of these things completely turned off the signals, they did reduce them to a point where I could get on with things and not spend time focusing on the signals. I have noticed that it seems to be worse when I have the time to sit and focus on it – then it is more difficult to get rid of it.
>
> There seemed to be a point where the handling techniques kicked in. The signals began to get shorter and shorter, less insistent, and the obsession which they normally produced, which required me to concentrate on them, began to subside until they were only there occasionally.
>
> My real problem had been with driving. I began to drive again in all types of situations. I am now at the point where I can drive unaccompanied on the motorway.
>
> I was glad we did not spend loads of time looking back into my past and asking what would have probably been fairly unfruitful questions about a past which could have been the cause of none or all of my problems and a few more.

The client described himself as 97 per cent recovered. His record of solutions, which he generated largely by himself, was a flexible repertoire he employed against panic attacks. He developed a 'firing order' in which he used them, as well as realising that nothing worked for long and that it was important for him to vary his strategies.

In his summary, he refers to what was for him a turning point – when he accepted the reframing of *symptoms* into *signals*, which required an active response from him. The reframing included an externalisation of his anxiety as something that attacked him (sometimes when he was in a kind of trance). He redefined his panic responses as signalling an attack, against which he could defend himself, rather than symptoms that implied an illness or condition over which he had little control. The client's attitude to medication enabled him to make the best possible use of the time to replace his old anxieties with 'activities' (his words), by which he meant strategies that he could continue to use once he had finished the medication.

FANTASY

A groupwork exercise that I have given a solution-focused slant to is called the Land of the Giants (original author unknown).

The facilitator invites the members of the group to imagine that they have arrived in a land where everyone else is a giant. Each person needs to work out how they will meet their basic survival needs.

Some people say that they would lead a clandestine life, coming out only at night to scavenge. Others would observe how the giants behave and then approach one who looks friendly. Others would visit places where giants who share the same interests as them might be found – for example, shopping malls, the gym, the pub – in the hope of finding a soul brother or sister there who liked little people!

Some participants feel confident that the giants will like them and they only need to ask for help and it will be forthcoming. Others think that they would need to plead for mercy or compassion, while others would try to impress the giants by presenting themselves as wise aliens with knowledge to share or fascinating creatures who could be entertaining court jesters.

When we debrief after the exercise, I begin by asking everyone whether or not they have ever been in a Land of Giants. Of course we have all had this experience as children, but people also mention times and situations in their lives when they felt small and powerless, such as when they were ill in hospital or started a new job or became a parent themselves. Talking about these times can be a powerful emotional experience that requires gentle support from the facilitator and the group, particularly if the cathartic situation was a traumatic one. Exploring the fantasy reveals strategies that clients currently use in their lives, as well as some that were useful in the past but are no longer appropriate. The exercise illuminates the clients' basic life stances.

From a solution-focused perspective, we explore:

- strategies that work for clients in the present
- strategies that no longer work
- qualities and strengths that the exercise has revealed
- past experiences that they can draw on to help them in the present
- small steps that they might take in the next few weeks to meet their needs and those of others.

Problem-solving techniques

IN A WORD

Lazarus' (1981) technique of inviting clients to state their problem in one word, then put it into the context of one sentence can be useful. The technique helps to give an immediate focus to the work and often reveals key feelings and concerns. Where possible, the practitioner will then tentatively convert the initial problem statement into a goal statement.

EXAMPLE

Practitioner: Could you put your problem into one or two words?
Client: Failure.
Practitioner: Could you put that into a sentence?
Client: The sentence would be 'I am a complete failure in making relationships with members of the opposite sex'.
Practitioner: So, up until now you feel that you have not had much success in these relationships and you would like to improve them. What will be the first signs for you that you are beginning to make better relationships?

FORCE-FIELD ANALYSIS

Egan (1990) incorporated this technique into his three-stage model of helping. Practitioner and client identify the positive and negative forces that are either facilitating or hindering the client from achieving her goals. Having identified and prioritised both sets of forces, they explore strategies to maximise the positives and minimise the negatives (see Figure 9.2).

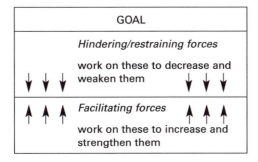

Figure 9.2   *Force-field analysis*

The forces restraining the client from achieving his goal might include the way in which he thinks about the problem, his attachment to failed solutions and fears that taking risks might make the situation worse. His social network may be a powerful reinforcer of these negative constraints. In order to develop facilitative strategies, the practitioner will help the client to find alternative ways of thinking about the problem and encourage and support him 'to do something different'. SFT reinforces facilitating processes by building on strengths and exceptions. It constantly seeks out resources, both personal and environmental, and stresses client competence. Unless this work is accomplished with a strong sense of realism, it may develop into myopic optimism, resulting in the client underestimating the difficulties involved in making changes and consequently giving up when change proves more difficult than anticipated. In my view, incorporating a negative focus into strategy-setting increases the realism with which the client tackles the problem. A solution-focused use of force-field analysis might employ some of the questions shown in Figure 9.3.

- When, where and how will obstacles arise to block you?
- What will be the first signs for you that you've met an obstacle?
- What do you think will be the hardest part of making these changes?
- What have you learned from your past experience of difficulties that will help you?
- How do you think other people will respond once you start to change?
- How will you remember what to do when you feel discouraged?
- What will you say to yourself at those times?
- Who would be a resource for you at that time?
- What would you do if you discovered that you take two steps forward then one step back?
- Do you think that your situation is as bad as it will get or do you think it could get worse?
- Even if you cannot solve the situation, what would you need to do to stop it getting worse?
- On a scale of zero to ten, ten being you are absolutely confident you can overcome these obstacles, where are you today and is that good enough?

Figure 9.3   *Solution-focused questions for force-field analysis*

There are, of course, some restraining structural forces over which the client has no control, such as economic policy and its effect on employment practices. However, even then, the client may find opportunities to join with others to work towards political and social change.

GENERATING SOLUTIONS

SFT encourages us to use our imagination – for example, in using the miracle question, predictions, rehearsals and visualisations. One of its strong points is its ability to generate solutions with clients and, for this to be effective, some ground rules are necessary. Here are some examples:

* write down every suggestion
* do not criticise any suggestion
* encourage quantity – evaluate quality later
* combine suggestions to make new ones
* when the list is complete, leave it on one side, then return to it later to add to it or refine it.

The two parties engage in uncensored, imaginative, freely associated ideas around solutions that can open up possibilities. The practitioner can help the client to refine the options by referring to previously unearthed exceptions and examples of client competence. Both can contribute to the exercise but the facilitator's principal role is to encourage and support the client.

What SFT can offer other traditions

If SFT can be enriched by integrating techniques from other traditions, what can SFT ideas and practices add to the work of practitioners from other traditions?

* SFT challenges practitioners to reconsider the balance between problem exploration and solution construction. Techniques such as scaling and the miracle question can help to free the process up when it has become enmeshed in problem-talk.
* Being curious about the client's coping strategies corrects the mindset that sees many clients as sick or inadequate. It can also act as an antidote to blinkered problem-focused thinking that minimises and dismisses the client's ingenuity and inventiveness.
* SFT reminds practitioners that assessment is not a neutral activity and that it is not always necessary to begin with history or search for causation.
* It privileges concrete descriptions of clients' experience, rather than professional-led definitions and diagnoses. It also encourages a 'matching' between client and counsellor communications.
* It fosters awareness of the social reality in which professional conversations take place. It highlights the power of language to negotiate multiple realities and increase the possibility of problem solving.
* It encourages practitioners to trust and respect their clients.
* It respects the rights of clients to shape their goals.
* Its flexibility regarding the length and frequency of sessions challenges practitioners who tend to see all clients weekly for a '50-minute hour'.

- Its minimalism reminds us about boundaries and the dangers of dependency.
- Its emphasis on the value of 'joining with' the client and not engaging in confrontational behaviour promotes creative ways of entering into the client's frame of reference.
- Many of the above ideas and practices can be integrated into other forms of helping without undermining the core beliefs of the practitioner.

10

Applying the Solution-focused Approach

Many practitioners have creatively adapted solution-focused ideas and practices to fit the needs of different client groups. These inspiring advocates of the approach work in a wide range of settings, such as education, business, criminal justice, substance misuse, health and social work. They are to be found in local authorities and voluntary organisations as well as the private sector. In this chapter, I will briefly touch on some of these areas.

Groupwork

The solution-focused literature describes groups for parents (Selekman, 1991), couples (Zimmerman, Prest and Wetzel, 1997), immigrants (Aambo, 1997), perpetrators of domestic violence (Uken and Sebold, 1996), patients (Hoskisson, 2003; Sharry, 2001; Vaughn, Hastings and Kassner, 1996), supervisees (Thomas, 1994) and staff (Goldberg and Szyndler, 1994). Some of the advantages for facilitators and members of SFT groups are:

- the emphasis on strengths, successes and compliments creates a non-blaming, positive climate in the group
- the affirmation of group members' achievements in the presence of their peers raises self-esteem
- the outward-looking, future-orientated approach of the group generates more energy and ideas than a problem-focused orientation.
- a group trained to look for exceptions and strengths can become a powerful source of social and moral support for the individual
- the specificity of goals, both for the members and the group as a whole, provides a focus for monitoring progress and avoids time-wasting irrelevancies
- the focus on small changes creates a positive momentum within the group
- the egalitarian nature of SFT encourages members to take responsibility for the group – the role of the leader is to ask questions rather than provide answers
- the active participation in other people's search for solutions can help each member to become more aware of their own solutions and it may be possible to borrow someone else's solution, too

- people who find it difficult to talk about their problems in front of others are often more willing to talk about solutions and the non-confrontational nature of an SFT group encourages open expression by its members
- the absence of analysis and interpretation reduces anxiety levels within the group
- the descriptive and concrete questions characteristic of SFT help to engage people who would struggle with abstract discussions
- there is an emphasis on utilising all the resources in the group and the group support and dynamic can help each individual to carry out tasks and counterbalance possible negative and pessimistic messages from other quarters
- groupwork often enhances experiential solution-focused exercises
- the rejection of labels and a wariness about diagnosis helps to remove the stigma of group membership – it is not a group for people with problems, but, rather, one for people looking for solutions
- The group can develop rituals for celebrating successes.

Figure 10.1 summarises the dynamic of groups run on solution-focused principles.

Solution-focused groups:

- create an expectation of change
- find different ways of describing and understanding problems and solutions
- enable members to encourage one another
- do something different when stuck
- begin with small steps towards change
- seek 'skeleton' solutions that fit many different situations
- focus on members' strengths, transferable skills and exceptions to the problems
- elicit descriptions, not definitions or diagnoses, of problems
- are goal-orienated
- believe in the clients and trust their expertise
- value each person's humanity and interdependency.

Figure 10.1   *The dynamic of solution-focused groups*

Sharry (2001), in his excellent book *Solution-Focused Groupwork*, describes in detail the principles, dynamics and stages of solution-focused groupwork. He graphically describes how a group that privileges solutions, optimism, members' strengths and goals liberates the individual from the oppression of negativity and failure. His book offers a clear guide to those wanting to start a solution-focused group.

Organisations

I have taught solution-focused skills to trade union shop stewards, employees at all levels in a company, managers, administrators, personnel officers, health and safety officers, and staff support teams. Solution-focused skills and values enhance the culture of the workplace and improve communication and problem-solving abilities. Solution-focused organisations display the characteristics listed in Figure 10.2

- There is shared vision.
- Management trusts the workforce, treats people well and creates a culture conducive to best endeavours.
- Develops employees' talents and expertise and builds on their strengths.
- Emphasises cooperation and collaboration between colleagues and departments.
- Consults at every level.
- Is always learning.
- Does what it can do best.
- Clearly defines aims and objectives
- Generates a creative atmosphere.
- Recognises and rewards employees' achievements.
- Encourages personal responsibility and stakeholding.
- Spends more time in solution construction than in problem exploration.
- Invests in the development of interpersonal communication skills.
- Runs purposeful and efficient meetings.

Figure 10.2   *Characteristics of solution-focused organisations*

Organisations can profitably explore the miracle question and scaling in relation to their core activities. Many organisations are hampered by what they have inherited or accumulated over the years. The miracle question enables staff to imagine how they would do things differently if they were to make a fresh start the following day. Moving between fantasy and reality, the miracle question minimises the negativity and lethargy that prevent people from believing that things could ever be different or better. The following questions can be helpful.

- If we come in to work tomorrow and the business/agency/organisation had been transformed overnight into the kind of organisation we would like to be, what would be the first signs we would notice?
- What would we be doing that was different?
- What would we have stopped doing?
- What would the miracle look like to senior management, middle management, project leaders, the cleaners, the personnel department, administration, the finance department?

- What difference would it make?
- How would our customers/users/clients notice the difference?
- How would it have come about?
- What would have been the first thing that would have changed?
- What would need to happen for some of those things to happen?
- Where would we start?
- What would be the gains for various people?
- Taking each aspect of the changes, on a scale of zero to ten, where are we now in relation to making them happen?
- Is that high enough for change to take place?
- Where do we want to get to?
- How could we move one point further up the scale?
- If one department moved up the scale, how would that affect other departments?

Teams

The solution-focused approach is a useful tool for building workplace teams. The positive emphasis that SFT places on agreed goals, encourages appreciation of colleagues, highlights the team's past successes and achievements and focuses on the team's preferred future and its unique strategies for getting there. SFT acts as an antidote to a blame culture, paralysis by problem analysis and conservative thinking, by minimising unproductive conflict arising from arguments about the past. It invites teams to 'do something different', helping them to escape the problem loop in which they find themselves.

SFT is not a threatening form of collaboration because it socialises team members to look for and draw attention to what is helpful and positive about what they, and their colleagues, are doing. A team steeped in solution-focused thinking can develop a powerful momentum for change.

Employee Assistance Programmes

The brief solution-focused model ideally suits the mushrooming Employee Assistance Programmes (EAPs) provided by many companies. These programmes typically offer a range of services to employees, from legal, financial and career advice, to critical incident debriefing and telephone and face-to-face counselling. Each EAP is different because of the differing needs of companies and the diversity of contracts. However, they share the common denominator of time-limited counselling, with four to eight sessions being typical. Short-term contracts carry the responsibility for the counsellors, whether they be employed in-house or by an external provider, to make maximum use of the available time. The key interventions required for this to happen are:

- thorough assessment
- rapid formation of the therapeutic alliance
- keeping close to the client's agenda
- focusing on a central issue
- realistic goal setting
- utilisation of the client's resources
- generation of problem-solving strategies
- evaluation of success
- planned endings.

SFT research (MacDonald, 1994; Kiser, 1988; De Jong and Hopwood, 1996) suggests that the typical number of sessions, even in settings where there is no rationing of services, is between three and six. This makes it an attractive model for workplace counsellors.

Most EAP clients present in crisis with specific work or personal issues, such as redundancy, workplace bullying or harassment, stress or personal relationship, health or life-event difficulties. In the main, they do not want long-term exploratory counselling. They need a skilled, non-judgemental and independent person with whom they can think through their situation and who will help them to decide what the most helpful plan might be. EAP clients are, therefore, well disposed towards solution construction as they have felt unable to find solutions on their own.

The fact that company contracts stipulate the number of sessions to which the client is entitled can provide a natural boundary for the work and spur the client on to invest time and energy in tackling it. When EAP counsellors cannot help clients within the limitations of the contract, they need to refer them to other sources of long-term or specialised help. To some extent, such cases should be identified at the assessment stage, but even cases that initially appear suitable for brief work can turn out to require more time than envisaged. The task is then to help the client to deal with the most pressing matters and identify areas that they would like to work on in another forum or at a later date. Although this sounds simple, the reality of such referrals can be difficult for the client, who feels reluctant to restart with another counsellor, and for the counsellor, who may feel frustrated, anxious and guilty about not completing the work with their client.

A more comprehensive description of how the solution-focused approach works in organisations and teams can be found in Jackson and McKergow's book *The Solutions Focus* (2002).

Education

Kral (1986), Durrant (1993b), Rhodes and Ajmal (1995) and others have written about using solution-focused ideas in consultations with teachers, school management and direct work with pupils. In my own experience, teachers, psychologists and educational social workers with large classes or caseloads, constantly dealing with crises with limited resources, have warmly welcomed the simplicity and discipline of SFT. Much of what SFT advocates is already being done by good educationalists. Figure 10.3 describes the characteristics of a solution-focused school (and the government policies behind it).

- Belief in the resourcefulness of its pupils.
- Commitment to the values of respect, diversity and fairness.
- Positive management of change.
- Acknowledgement of the contributions made by all staff and pupils.
- Genuine collaboration and partnership in learning.
- Commitment to empowering pupils by imparting the key skills of numeracy, literacy and IT.
- A vision of the school as part of the local community, involving parents, community groups, local businesses and others who can contribute to the life of the school.
- Culture of accountability and responsibility, but avoidance of blame and destructive criticism.
- Clear targets and goals for staff, pupils and the school as an organisation.
- Open, fair and realistic appraisal and auditing systems.
- Whole-school anti-bullying policy and use of peer counsellors.
- Effects liaison with other professional groups, such as social workers and psychologists.
- Wide use of devolved powers.
- Use of experienced and skilled teachers to facilitate colleagues' searches for solutions.

Figure 10.3   *Characteristics of a solution-focused school*

Student counselling services in colleges and universities are increasingly recognising that a high proportion of their clients attend for fewer than six sessions and so their counsellors need to be trained in brief work.

As a tutor in a college of higher education, I found that solution-focused ideas were very helpful in tutorials and seminars with students. All my students were mature students returning to study after a long break or had no previous experience of academic work at tertiary level. Aspects of the academic or clinical work often brought a temporary loss of confidence, power and status, with resulting confusion, anxiety, anger and fear.

A solution-focused perspective, while validating students' anxieties and fears, builds respectfully on the experiences, values, skills and learning styles that they bring to their learning. It helps them to formulate realistic learning objectives. Its attention to microplanning is useful when organising study patterns or writing essays. It is helpful for reducing perceived mountains into small hills, to be scaled one at a time. It reminds the tutor of the importance of giving constructive and encouraging feedback to students while at the same time 'joining with' them to find ways forward for further improvement. When solution-focused ideas permeate an entire course, it becomes a learning community in which there is a sense of partnership characterised by energy, purpose and mutual respect.

Health

Health workers, such as community psychiatric nurses, clinical psychologists, nurse therapists and counsellors in primary care, as well as others working in the voluntary sector, have shown considerable enthusiasm for using solution-focused ideas with patients with mental or physical illnesses (Webster, 1990; Twyn, 1992; Mason, Breen and Whipple, 1994; Vaughn, Cox Young, Webster and Thomas, 1996; Hawkes, 2003).

SFT beliefs and methods challenge the construction of medical labels and instead emphasise the active change-agent role that patients can play in managing their illness. SFT champions the individual's unique and changing experience of illness and seeks to utilise people's powers heal themselves.

Goldberg and Szyndler (1994) describe how staff in a paediatric ward used the method to generate an increased number of solutions. This was accomplished by building on the staff's knowledge and skills base and by increasing the variety of their interactions with patients, families and colleagues. According to Vaughn, Cox Young, Webster and Thomas (1996: 102):

> Solution-focused therapy is consistent with the aims of nursing interventions, including building clients' trust, promoting their sense of control and positive orientation, affirming and supporting their strengths, and setting health-oriented mutual goals.

A solution-focused approach to health adopts an 'holistic' stance that links body, mind and spirit with the social environment. An holistic approach taps the patients' unused or underused resources. Dodd (2003) argues that the values of a solution-focused approach connect with the deep human needs of people with mental illness.

SFT can be used with patients suffering from physical or mental problems. Its attention to small steps makes it user-friendly for patients with chronic or terminal illnesses. There are elements in any illness over which patients have no control and with which they need to come to terms, but there are others that invite a more active response.

The practitioner attempts to discover what patients are or are not doing when the pain is less acute (exceptions) and what the patients are already doing that is helpful or at least prevents the illness from getting worse (coping strategies). Patients may have psychological resources (thought stopping, diversionary thoughts, visualisations) of which they are unaware and that they can helpfully employ to divert negative thoughts. How people understand and relate to their illness or pain and how they and others construct their 'sick' role are crucial determinants in how they cope.

Scaling is a useful tool in helping to identify realistic goals and monitoring micro-steps towards their goals. With terminally ill patients, it may be helpful to omit the use of the word 'miracle' when asking future-focused questions. An alternative might be, 'When you were asleep, something happened that made you realise you were managing your situation as best you can given the circumstances. What would be the first signs for you that this had happened?' Using the traditional form of the miracle question might, however, be therapeutic for some clients. Although one answer to it might be an unattainable cure, there will inevitably be helpful things that the client would like to do or want others to do or refrain from doing. When people are terminally ill, they may have clear, strong ideas about how the precious remaining time they have should be spent.

Social work

There are many difficult issues to be resolved in the interface between the statutory roles of the social worker and the need for families and children to participate in genuinely therapeutic work that requires much lengthier treatment than this book allows. Solution-focused ideas are being used by social workers (George, Iveson and Ratner, 1990; Wheeler, 2003) who provide direct services to families, young people and children. They have been used in residential work (Durrant, 1993a), child protection (Turnell and Edwards, 1999) and with survivors of abuse (Dolan, 1991; McConkey, 1992). The solution-focused approach has much to offer social workers, including:

- its solution-orientated questions that can help to shift a potentially overwhelming pre-occupation with problems into more productive areas
- its descriptive language, which is useful when defining a focal issue and agreeing realistic goals
- a step-by-step approach, which helps to guide workers and clients through a maze of interconnected multiple problems
- it draws attention to the fact that clients have survived previous crises and attempts to discover how they coped and whether or not they could reactivate those strategies
- it is a respectful approach utilising clients' strengths, skills and values
- an emphasis on collaboration and empowerment, which reduces hostility and resistance
- it has practical tools for use with involuntary and absent clients.

In the field of child protection, Turnell and Edwards (1999) have developed a 'signs of safety' programme that achieves the difficult balance between building co-operation while avoiding professional naïvety. Wheeler (2003) describes how the inclusivity of the approach helps to develop collaboration with clients, acknowledge their struggles and empower their strengths and skills. Wheeler (2003: 116) claims that, within social work in the UK, 'solution-focused practice is coming to be known as an approach which gets results, both good outcomes for service users and a sense of achievement for those working with them.'

Dolan (1991: 25) has developed a practical, sensitive and imaginative solution-focused approach to working with survivors of abuse. In her view, as well as listening and acknowledging the client's story:

> It is equally important that therapy not be limited to the tasks of recounting the details of the abuse and sorting out and acknowledging the resultant feelings. In order to respectfully and effectively address the client's treatment needs, therapy needs to include and strongly emphasise an active utilisation of the client's present life resources and images of future goals and possibilities.

Dolan (1991: 32) uses a solution-focused recovery scale that lists many ordinary day-to-day activities in which the client is engaged that are signs of healing as well as defining realistic goals.

Conclusion

Solution-focused thinking and practice continue to find new audiences, attracted by its optimism, simplicity and power. It is well on its way to becoming a major figure in the therapeutic arena. Among its practitioners are many talented, innovative and skilled people who co-create life-transforming experiences for their clients and, in so doing, empower them in new and unimagined ways. For my own part, discovering this respectful and life-affirming way of working has been the most significant event in my professional life. I will always be grateful for what it has taught me, personally and professionally.

What I, and other solution-focused practitioners, most value is that clients are centre stage. They are the real solution-focused practitioners!

Appendix: Solution-focused Resources

Training in the solution-focused approach

Focus on Solutions Limited
Bill O'Connell
Director of Training
97 Glyn Farm Road
Quinton
Birmingham B32 1NJ
0121 422 2525
www.focusonsolutions.co.uk
An Independent Training Organisation which specialises in the Solution-Focused approach to Personal and Organisational change. Mainly provides in-house training for organisations.

The Brief Therapy Practice
7–8 Newbury Street
London EC1A 7HU
020 7600 3366
solutions@brieftherapy.org.uk
www.brieftherapy.org.uk
Organises presentations by international figures in the Solution-Focused field and runs an extensive training programme.

The University of Birmingham offers a Masters course in Solution-Focused Therapy, delivered partly over the internet. For further information, consult its website at www.bham.ac.uk

Websites

International
www.brief-therapy.org
The Brief Family Therapy Center in Milwaukee USA and the home of solution-focused brief therapy. Here you will find Steve de Shazer's 'Current Thoughts' and Insoo Kim Berg's 'Hot tips' and 'Students' Corner'.

www.ukasfp.co.uk
Website for the United Kingdom Association of Solution Focused Practice formed in 2003 to promote solution-focused work in the United Kingdom. Runs an annual conference and is developing a network of practitioners to exchange ideas for good practice, as well as exploring professional issues such as accreditation.

www.ebta.nu
Website for the European Brief Therapy Association. This provides an ever-growing collection of research, articles and information on the annual conferences.

www.enabling.org/ia/sft
The solution-focused therapy discussion list is a lively virtual community engaged in discussing various aspects of solution-focused brief therapy, sharing ideas, answering each other's questions and sharing a degree of irreverence. The list operates via e-mail. The solution-focused therapy page includes information about the list as well as other details.

www.brieftherapynetwork.com
The Canadian network for solution-focused practitioners. This ever-growing website includes a useful collection of articles and interviews. BTN has a discussion forum facility.

www.reteaming.com
Ben Furman and Tapani Ahola's Helsinki Brief Therapy Institute website, which illustrates the various adaptations of solution-talk and reteaming. Those who work with children will find Ben's 'Kids' Skills' section to be of particular relevance, along with 'The Steps of Responsibility: How to Deal with the Wrongdoings of Children and Adolescents in a Way That Builds Their Sense of Responsibility'.

www.talkingcure.com
Website for Scott Miller, Barry Duncan and Mark Hubble and their Institute for the Study of Therapeutic Change. Includes summaries of the latest published research in therapy outcomes across the broad range of therapeutic approaches. Their concern is with 'what works in therapy'. The site features a particularly interesting baloney watch.

http://brieftherapy.com
Website for Bill O'Hanlon. Bill's site explains his particular slant on solution-focused work and includes an attic with various handouts and lists.

www.brieftherapysydney.com.au
Website for Michael Durrant's Brief Therapy Institute of Sydney. The site includes a useful collection of articles and the most comprehensive collection of links you are likely to find, running like a timeline of SFT.

http://porodwyk.republika.pl/angielski.htm
Website for Tomasz Switek in Poland. Tomasz has famously contributed to the SF world by producing his Deck of Trumps, which can be found on

this website. The site also includes the research into the personal impact of becoming a SF practitioner.

www.gingerich.net
The SFBT part of Wally Gingerich's home page provides an impressive collection of research into the effectiveness of SFBT and information on the MAM, an assessment tool designed to explore the solution-focused dimensions of team discussions.

United Kingdom
www.focusonsolutions.co.uk
Homepage for Focus on Solutions Limited, the Director of Training of which is Bill O'Connell.

www.solutionfocusedpractice.com
Homepage for Steve Conlon, a family therapist.

www.brieftherapy.org.uk
Homepage for Brief, also known as the Brief Therapy Practice, in London. The site keeps up-to-date information about its training courses and workshops. It also has an interesting section on practice notes.

www.yorkshiresolutions.org.uk
A professional interest group, open to anyone who uses solution-focused therapy (SFT) in the region. It meets five times a year, in Leeds, to exchange ideas, share training and offers mutual support to those who come along with their SFT work.

www.psychsft.freeserve.co.uk
Dr Alasdair Macdonald's homepage. As research coordinator for EBTA, Alasdair has amassed a wealth of research on SFBT.

www.thesolutionsfocus.com
Website for The Solutions Focus group in Cheltenham. Mark McKergow and Paul Z. Jackson mainly use a SF approach with organisations. The site provides information on the foundations of their work and training events, along with a collection of articles, tips and examples.

www.sycol.org
Website for Ioan Rees and colleagues. Provides information on training events and workshops.

References

Aambo, A. (1997) 'Tasteful solutions: solution-focused work with groups of immigrants', *Contemporary Family Therapy*, 19 (1) March: 63–79.

Adams, J., Piercy, F. and Jurich, J. (1991) 'Effects of solution focused therapy's "formula first session task" on compliance and outcome in family therapy', *Journal of Marital and Family Therapy*, 17 (3): 277–90.

Adler, A. (1925) *The Practice and Theory of Individual Psychology*. London: Routledge & Kegan Paul.

Alexander, F. and French, T.M. (1946) *Psychoanalytic Therapy*. New York: Ronald Press.

Allen, J. (1993) 'The constructionist paradigm: values and ethics', in J. Laird (ed.), *Revisioning Social Work Education: A Social Constructionist Approach*. New York: Haworth Press.

Anderson, H. and Swim, S. (1995) 'Supervision as collaborative conversation: connecting the voices of supervisor and supervisee', *Journal of Systemic Therapies*, 14 (2): 1–13.

Ardrey, R. (1970) *The Social Contract: A Personal Enquiry into the Evolutionary Sources of Order and Disorder*. New York: Athenaeum.

Bachelor, A. (1988) 'How clients perceive therapist empathy', *Psychotherapy*, 25: 227–40.

Bailey-Martiniere, L. (1993) 'Solution-oriented psychotherapy – the "difference" for female clients', *News of the Difference*, II (2): 10–12.

Bandler, R. and Grinder, J. (1979) *Frogs into Princes*. Moab, Utah: Real People Press.

Barkham, M. (1993) 'Counselling for a brief period', in W. Dryden (ed.), *Questions and Answers for Counselling in Action*. London: Sage.

Barret-Kruse, C. (1994) 'Brief counselling: a user's guide for traditionally trained counsellors', *International Journal for the Advancement of Counselling*, 17: 109–15.

Bateson, G. (1972) *Steps to an Ecology of Mind*. New York: Ballantine.

Berg, I.K. (1991) *Family Preservation: A Brief Therapy Workbook*. London: Brief Therapy Press.

Berg, I.K. (1994) *Family Based Services*. New York: W.W. Norton.

Berg, I.K. and de Shazer, S. (1993) 'Making numbers talk: language in therapy', in S. Freedman (ed.), *New Language of Change*. New York: Guilford Press.

Berg, I.K. and Miller, S.D. (1992) *Working with the Problem Drinker: A Solution Focused Approach*. New York: W.W. Norton.

Beutler, L. and Crago, M. (1987) 'Strategies and techniques of prescriptive psychotherapeutic intervention', in R. Hales and A. Frances (eds), *Psychiatric Updates: The American Psychiatric Association Annual Review*. Washington: American Psychiatric Press.

Bischof, G. (1993) 'Solution-focused brief therapy and experiential family therapy activities: an integration', *Journal of Systemic Therapies*, 12 (3): 61–72.

Bloom, B.L. (1992) *Planned Short Term Psychotherapy*. Boston, Massachusetts: Allyn & Bacon.

Bond, T. (1993) *Standards and Ethics for Counselling in Action*. London: Sage.

Bramwell, S. (2003) Personal communication.

Brech, J. and Agulnik, P. (1996) 'Do brief interventions reduce waiting times for counselling?', *Counselling*, 7 (4): 322–6.

British Association for Counselling (1996) *Code of Ethics and Practice for Counsellors*. Rugby: BAC.

British Association for Counselling and Psychotherapy (2003) *Ethical Framework for Good Practice in Counselling and Psychotherapy*. Rugby: BACP.

Brown, S.D. and Lent, R.W. (1992) *Handbook of Counselling Psychology*. New York: Wiley.

Budman, S.H. and Gurman, A. (1988) *Theory and Practice of Brief Therapy*. New York: Guilford Press.

Butler, W. and Powers, K. (1996) 'Solution-focused grief therapy', in S. Miller, M. Hubble and B. Duncan (eds), *Handbook of Solution-Focused Brief Therapy*. San Francisco: Jossey-Bass.

Cade, B. and O'Hanlon, W. (1993) *A Brief Guide to Brief Therapy*. New York: W.W. Norton.

Cantwell, P. and Holmes, S. (1995) 'Cumulative process: a collaborative approach to systemic supervision', *Journal of Systemic Therapies*, 14 (2): 35–46.

Chevalier, A.J. (1995) *On the Client's Path: A Manual for the Practice of Solution-Focused Therapy*. Oakland, California: New Harbinger.

Collar, C. (2004) Personal communication.

Cummings, N. and Sayama, M. (1995) *Focused Psychotherapy*. New York: Brunner/Mazel.

Darmody, M. (2003) 'A solution-focused approach to sexual trauma', in B. O'Connell and S. Palmer, *Handbook of Solution-Focused Therapy*. London: Sage.

Davanloo, H. (ed.) (1980) *Short Term Dynamic Psychotherapy*. New York: Jason Aronson.

De Jong, P. and Hopwood, L. (1996) 'Outcome research on treatment conducted at the Brief Family Therapy Center, 1992–3', in S. Miller, M. Hubble and B. Duncan (eds), *Handbook of Solution-Focused Brief Therapy*. San Francisco: Jossey-Bass.

de Shazer, S. (1984) 'The death of resistance', *Family Process*, 23: 11–17.

de Shazer, S. (1985) *Keys to Solutions in Brief Therapy*. New York: W.W. Norton.

de Shazer, S. (1988) *Clues: Investigating Solutions in Brief Therapy*. New York: W.W. Norton.

de Shazer, S. (1994) *Words were Originally Magic*. New York: W.W. Norton.

de Shazer, S. (1996) Presentation on solution-focused therapy, Glasgow, organised by the Brief Therapy Practice.

de Shazer, S. (1998) *The Right Path or the Other Path?*, Brief Family Therapy Centre (video). Milwaukee: Brief Therapy Practice.

de Shazer, S. and Berg, I.K. (1992) 'Doing therapy: a post-structural re-vision', *Journal of Marital and Family Therapy*, 18 (1): 71–81.

de Shazer, S. and Berg, I.K. (1997) '"What works?" Remarks on research aspects of solution-focused therapy', *Journal of Family Therapy*, 19: 121–4.

de Shazer, S., Berg, I.K., Lipchik, E., Nunnally, E., Molnar, A., Gingerich, W. and Weiner-Davis, M. (1986) 'Brief therapy: focused solution development', *Family Process*, 25: 207–21.

de Shazer, S. and Molnar, A. (1984) 'Four useful interventions in brief family therapy', *Journal of Marital and Family Therapy*, 10 (3): 297–304.

Dodd, T. (2003) 'Solution-focused therapy in mental health', in B. O'Connell and S. Palmer, *Handbook of Solution-Focused Therapy*. London: Sage.

Dolan, Y. (1991) *Resolving Sexual Abuse: Solution-Focused Therapy and Ericksonian Hypnosis for Adult Survivors*. New York: W.W. Norton.

Dolan, Y. (1998) *One Small Step*. Watsonville, California: Papier-Mache Press.

Duncan, B. (1992) 'Strategic therapy, eclecticism and the therapeutic relationship', *Journal of Marital and Family Therapy*, 18 (1): 17–24.

Durrant, M. (1993a) *Residential Treatment: A Co-operative Competency-based Approach to Therapy and Program Design*. New York: W.W. Norton.

Durrant, M. (1993b) *Creative Strategies for School Problems*. Epping, New South Wales: Eastwood Family Therapy Centre.

Durrant, M. (1997) Presentation on brief solution-focused therapy, London, organised by the Brief Therapy Practice.

Eckert, P. (1993) 'Acceleration of change: catalysts in brief therapy', *Clinical Psychology Review*, 13: 241–53.

Egan, G. (1990) *The Skilled Helper*. 4th edn. Pacific Grove, California: Brooks/Cole.

Eliot, T.S. (1963) *Collected Poems 1909–1962*. London: Faber & Faber.

Erickson, M.H. (1980) *Collected Papers*. Vols 1–4 (E. Rossi, ed.). New York: Irvington.

Fanger, M. (1993) 'After the shift: time effective treatment in the possibility frame', in S. Friedman (ed.), *The New Language of Change*. New York: Guilford Press.

Ferenczi, S. and Rank, O. (1925) *The Development of Psychoanalysis*. New York: Dover.

Fisch, R. (1994) 'Basic elements in the brief therapies', in M. Hoyt (ed.), *Constructive Therapies*. New York: Guilford Press.

Fisch, R., Weakland, J.H. and Segal, L. (1982) *The Tactics of Change: Doing Therapy Briefly*. San Francisco: Jossey-Bass.

Frances, A., Clarkin, J. and Perry, S. (1984) *Differential Therapeutics in Psychiatry: The Art and Science of Treatment Selection*. New York: Brunner/Mazel.

Freedman, J. and Combs, G. (1993) 'Invitations to new stories: using questions to explore alternative possibilities', in S. Gilligan and R. Price (eds), *Therapeutic Conversations*. New York: W.W. Norton.

Gale, J. and Newfield, N. (1992) 'A conversation analysis of a solution-focused marital therapy session', *Journal of Marital and Family Therapy*, 18 (2): 153–65.

Garfield, S.L. and Bergin, A.E. (1994) *Handbook of Psychotherapy and Behavioral Change*. New York: Wiley.

Gelatt H.B. (1989) 'Positive uncertainty: a new decision-making framework for counselling', *Journal of Counselling Psychology*, 36: 252–6.

George, E., Iveson, C. and Ratner, H. (1990) *Problem to Solution*. London: BT Press.

Gingerich, W.J. and Eisengart, S. (2000) 'Solution-focused brief therapy: a review of the outcome research', *Family Process*, 39: 477–98.

Goldberg, D. and Szyndler, J. (1994) 'Debating solutions: a model for teaching about psychosocial issues', *Journal of Family Therapy*, 16: 209–17.

Hanton, P. (2003) 'Solution-focused therapy and substance misuse', in B. O'Connell and S. Palmer, *Handbook of Solution-Focused Therapy*. London: Sage.

Hawkes, D. (2003) 'A solution-focused approach to "Psychosis"', in B. O'Connell and S. Palmer, *Handbook of Solution-Focused Therapy*. London: Sage.

Hawkes, D., Marsh, T.I. and Wilgosh, R. (1998) *Solution Focused Therapy: A Handbook for Health Care Professionals*. Oxford: Butterworth Heinemann.

Hoskisson, P. (2003) 'Solution-focused groupwork', in B. O'Connell and S. Palmer, *Handbook of Solution-Focused Therapy*. London: Sage.

Howard, K.I., Kopta, S., Krause, M. and Orlinsky, D. (1986) 'The dose effect relationship in psychotherapy', *American Psychologist*, 41: 159–64.

Hoyt, M. (1995) *Brief Therapy and Managed Care*. San Francisco: Jossey-Bass.

Hudson, P. and O'Hanlon, W. (1991) *Rewriting Love Stories*. New York: W.W. Norton.

Hutchins, D.E. (1989) 'Improving the counselling relationship', in W. Dryden (ed.), *Key Issues for Counselling in Action*. London: Sage.

Inskipp, F. (1996) 'New directions in supervision', in R. Bayne, I. Horton and J. Bunrose (eds), *New Directions in Counselling*. London: Routledge.

Inskipp, F. and Proctor, B. (1989) *Being Supervised: Audio tape 1: Principles of Counselling*. St Leonard's-on-Sea: Alexia Publications.

Iveson, C. (2003) 'Solution-focused couples counselling', in B. O'Connell and S. Palmer, *Handbook of Solution-Focused Therapy*. London: Sage.

Jackson, P.Z. and McKergow, M. (2002) *The Solutions Focus*. London. Nicholas Brealey.

Jacob, F. (2001) *Solution-Focused Recovery from Eating Distress*. London: Brief Therapy Press.

Keen, S. (2003) Personal communication.

Kelly, G.A. (1955) *The Psychology of Personal Constructs*. New York: W.W. Norton.

Kiser, D. (1988) 'A follow-up study conducted at the Brief Family Therapy Center'. Unpublished manuscript.

Kiser, D. and Nunnally, E. (1990) 'The relationship between treatment length and goal achievement in solution-focused therapy'. Unpublished manuscript.

Kiser, D., Piercy, F. and Lipchik, E. (1993) 'The integration of emotion in solution-focused therapy', *Journal of Marital and Family Therapy*, (19) 3: 233–42.

Kleckner, T., Frank, L., Bland, C., Amendt, J. and Du Ree Bryant, R. (1992) 'The myth of the unfeeling strategic therapist', *Journal of Marital and Family Therapy*, 18 (1): 41–51.

Kogan, L.S. (1957) 'The short-term case in a family agency', *Social Casework*, 38: 366–74.

Koss, M.P. and Butcher, J.N. (1986) 'Research on brief psychotherapy', in S.L. Garfield and A.E. Begin (eds), *Handbook of Psychotherapy and Behavior Change*, 3rd edn. New York: Wiley.

Kral, R. (1986) 'Indirect therapy in schools', in S. de Shazer and R. Kral (eds), *Indirect Approaches in Therapy*. Rockville, Massachusetts: Aspen.

Kral, R. and Kowalski, K. (1989) 'After the miracle: the second stage in solution-focused brief therapy', *Journal of Strategic and Systemic Therapies*, 8 (2): 73–6.

Lambert, M. (1986) 'Implications of psychotherapy outcome research for eclectic psychotherapy', in J. Norcross (ed.), *Handbook of Eclectic Psychotherapy*. New York: Brunner/Hazel. pp. 436–62.

Lankton, S.R. (1990) 'Ericksonian strategic therapy', in J.K. Zeig and W.W. Munion (eds), *What is Psychotherapy? Contemporary Perspectives*. San Francisco: Jossey-Bass.

Lawson, D. (1994) 'Identifying pre-treatment change', *Journal of Counselling and Development*, 72: 244–8.

Lazarus, A. (1981) *The Practice of Multimodal Therapy*. New York: McGraw-Hill.

Leem M-Y. (1999) 'A model for short-term solution-focused group treatment of male domestic violence offenders', *Journal of Family Social Work*. 3 (2): 39–57.

Lethem, J. (1994) *Moved to Tears, Moved to Action: Solution-Focused Brief Therapy with Women and Children*. London: Brief Therapy Press.

Lindforss, L. and Magnusson, D. (1997) 'Solution-focused therapy in prison', *Contemporary Family Therapy*, 19: 89–104.

Lipchik, E. (1991) 'Spouse abuse: challenging the party line', *The Family Therapy Networker*, 15: 59–63.

Lipchik, E. and de Shazer, S. (1986) 'The purposeful interview', *Journal of Strategic and Family Therapies*, 5 (1): 88–9.

Lipchik, E. and Kubicki, A.D. (1996) 'Solution-focused domestic violence views: bridges toward a new reality in couples therapy', in S. Miller, M. Hubble and B. Duncan (eds), *Handbook of Solution-Focused Brief Therapy*. San Francisco: Jossey-Bass.

Llewelyn, S.P. (1988) 'Psychological therapy as viewed by clients and therapists', *British Journal of Clinical Psychology*, 27: 223–37.

Lynch, G. (1996) 'What is truth? A philosophical introduction to counselling research', *Counselling*, (7) 2: 144–8.

Macdonald, A.J. (1994) 'Brief therapy in adult psychiatry', *Journal of Family Therapy*, 16: 415–26.

Macdonald, A.J. (2003) 'Research in solution-focused brief therapy', in B. O'Connell and S. Palmer, *Handbook of Solution-Focused Therapy*. London: Sage.

Malan, D.H. (1963) *A Study of Brief Psychotherapy*. New York: Plenum.

Malan, D.H. (1976) *The Frontier of Brief Psychotherapy*. New York: Plenum.

Malan, D., Heath, E., Bacal, H. and Balfour, F. (1975) 'Psychodynamic changes in untreated neurotic patients. II. Apparently genuine improvements', *Archives of General Psychiatry*, 32: 110–26.

Mann, J. (1973) *Time Limited Psychotherapy*. Cambridge, Massachusetts: Harvard University Press.

Manthei, R.J. (1996) 'A follow-up study of clients who fail to begin counselling or terminate after one session', *International Journal for the Advancement of Counselling*, 18: 115–28.

Mason, W.H., Breen, R.Y. and Whipple, W.R. (1994) 'Solution-focused therapy and inpatient psychiatric nursing', *Nursing*, 32 (10): 46–9.

McConkey, N. (1992) 'Working with adults to overcome the effects of sexual abuse: integrating solution-focused therapy, systems thinking and gender issues', *Journal of Strategic and Systemic Therapies*, 11 (3): 4–18.

McKeel, A. and Weiner-Davis, M. (1995) 'Pre-suppositional questions and pretreatment change: a further analysis'. Unpublished manuscript.

Melchior, G. (2003) Personal communication.

Merl, H. (1995) 'Reflecting supervision', *Journal of Systemic Therapies*, 14 (2): 47–56.

Merry, T. (1990) 'Client-centred therapy: some trends and some troubles', *Counselling*, 1 (1): 17–18.

Miller, S. (1992) 'The symptoms of solutions', *Journal of Strategic and Systemic Therapies*, 11 (1): 1–11.

Miller, S. (1994) 'The solution conspiracy: a mystery in three instalments', *Journal of Systemic Therapies*, 13 (1): 18–37.

Norman, H. (2003) 'Solution-focused reflecting teams', in B. O'Connell and S. Palmer, *Handbook of Solution-Focused Therapy*. London: Sage.

Nunnally, E. and Lipchik, E. (1989) 'Some uses of writing in solution-focused brief therapy', *Journal of Independent Social Work*, 4: 5–19.

Nylund, D. and Corsiglia, V. (1994) 'Becoming solution-focused in brief therapy: remembering something we already know', *Journal of Systema Therapies*, 13 (1): 5–11.

O'Connell, B. (1997) 'A grounded theory approach to solution-focused therapy'. M.Sc. dissertation, unpublished.

O'Connell, B. (2001) *Solution Focused Stress Counselling*. London: Continuum.

O'Connell, B. and Palmer, S. (2003) *Handbook of Solution-Focused Therapy*. London: Sage.

O'Connell, M.F. (1997) 'Ideas for therapy'. Personal communication.

O'Hanlon, B. and Beadle, S. (1994) *A Field Guide to Possibility Land: Possibility Therapy Methods*. Omaha, Nebraska: Possibility Press.

O'Hanlon, B. and Weiner-Davis, M. (1989) *In Search of Solutions*. New York: W.W. Norton.

O'Hanlon, B. and Wilk, J. (1987) *Shifting Contexts*. New York: Guilford Press.

Payne, M. (1993) 'Down-under innovation: a bridge between person-centred and systemic models', *Counselling*, 4 (2): 117–19.

Pekarik, G. (1991) 'Relationship of expected and actual treatment duration for adult and child clients', *Journal of Clinical Child Psychology*, 23: 121–5.

Pekarik, G. and Wierzbicki, J. (1986) 'The relationship between clients' expected and actual treatment duration', *Psychotherapy*, 23: 532–4.

Perry, S. (1987) 'The choice of duration and frequency for outpatient psychotherapy', *Annual Review*, 6.

Prochaska, J.O., Di Clemente, C.C. and Norcross, J.C. (1992) 'In search of how people change', *American Psychologist*, 47: 1102–14.

Quick, E. (1994) 'From unattainable goals to achievable solutions', *Journal of Systemic Therapies*, 13 (2): 59–64.

Ratner, H. (2003) 'Solution-focused therapy in schools', in B. O'Connell and S. Palmer, *Handbook of Solution-Focused Therapy*. London: Sage.

Rhodes, J. and Ajmal, Y. (1995) *Solution-Focused Thinking in Schools*. London: BT Press.

Rilke, R.M. (1990) *Peacemaking: Day by Day: Daily Readings*. London: Pax Christi.

Rogers, C. (1961) *On Becoming a Person*. London: Constable.

Rosenbaum, R., Hoyt, M. and Talmon, M. (1990) 'The challenge of single-session therapies: creating pivotal moments', in R. Wells and V. Gianetti (eds), *The Handbook of Brief Therapies*. New York: Plenum.

Rossi, E. (ed.) (1980) *Collected Papers of Milton Erickson on Hypnosis*. Vol. 4. New York: Irvington.

Russell, R. (1989) 'Language and psychotherapy', *Clinical Psychology Review*, 9: 505–19.

Ryle, A. (1991) *Cognitive-Analytic Therapy: Active Participation in Change*. Chichester: Wiley.

Schapp, C., Bennun, I., Schindler, L. and Hoogduin, K. (1993) *Therapeutic Relationship in Behavioural Psychotherapy*. Chichester: Wiley.

Schwartz, D.P. (1955) 'Has family therapy reached the stage where it can appreciate the concept of stages?', in J. Breunlin (ed.), *Stages: Patterns of Change over Time*. Rockville, Massachusetts: Aspen.

Segal, L. (1986) *The Dream of Reality: Heinz Von Foerster's Constructivism*. New York: W.W. Norton.

Selekman, M. (1991) 'The solution-oriented parenting group: a treatment alternative that works', *Journal of Strategic and Systemic Therapies*, 10 (1): 36–48.

Selekman, M. and Todd, T. (1995) 'Co-creating a context for change in the supervisory system: the solution focused supervision model', *Journal of Systemic Therapies*, 14 (3): 21–33.

Sharry, J. (2001) *Solution-Focused Groupwork*. London: Sage.

Sharry, J. (2003) 'Solution-focused parent training', in B. O'Connell and S. Palmer, *Handbook of Solution-Focused Therapy*. London: Sage.

Sifneos, P.E. (1979) *Short-Term Dynamic Psychotherapy*. New York: Plenum.

Skott-Myhre, H. (1992) *Competency-Based Counseling: Basic Principles and Assumptions*. Santa Fe: Further Institute Press.

Slive, A., MacLaurin, B., Oakander, M. and Amundson, J. (1995) 'Walk-in single sessions: a new paradigm in clinical service delivery', *Journal of Systemic Therapies*, 14 (1): 3–11.

Smith, M.L. (1980) *The Benefits of Psychotherapy*. Baltimore, Maryland: Johns Hopkins University.

Steenbarger, B. (1994) 'Toward science–practice integration in brief counselling and therapy', *The Counseling Psychologist*, 20 (3): 403–50.

Stern, S. (1993) 'Managed care, brief therapy, and therapeutic integrity', *Psychotherapy*, 30 (1): 162–75.

Street, E. and Downey, J. (1996) *Brief Therapeutic Consultations*. Chichester: Wiley.

Sundmann, P. (1997) 'Solution-focused ideas in social work', *Journal of Family Therapy*, 19: 159–172.

Talmon, M. (1990) *Single Session Therapy*. San Francisco: Jossey-Bass.

Talmon, M. (1996) 'Presentation on single-session therapy', London, organised by the Brief Therapy Practice.

Taylor, C. (1985) 'Theories of meaning', in C. Taylor (ed.), *Human Agency and Language*. Cambridge: Cambridge University Press.

Thomas, F. (1994) 'Solution-oriented supervision: the coaxing of expertise', *The Family Journal*, 2 (1): 11–17.

Ticho, E.A. (1972) 'Termination of psychoanalysis: treatment goals and life goals', *Psychoanalysis Quarterly*, 41: 315–33.

Twyn, L. (1992) 'Solution-oriented therapy and Rogerian Nursing Science: an integrated approach', *Archives in Psychiatric Nursing*, 6 (2): 83–9.

Turnell, A. and Edwards, S. (1999) *Signs of Safety: A Solution and Safety Oriented Approach to Child Protection Casework*. New York: W.W. Norton.

Uken, A. and Sebold, J. (1996) 'The Plumas Project: a solution-focused goal-directed domestic violence diversion program', *Journal of Collaborative Therapies*, 4: 10–17.

Vaughn, K., Hastings, G. and Kassner, C. (1996) 'Solution-oriented inpatient group therapy', *Journal of Systemic Therapies*, 15 (3): 1–14.

Vaughn, K., Cox Young, B., Webster, D.C. and Thomas, M.R. (1996) 'Solution-focused work in the hospital', in S. Miller, M. Hubble and B. Duncan (eds), *Handbook of Solution-Focused Brief Therapy*. San Francisco: Jossey-Bass.

Walter, J. and Peller, J. (1996) 'Assuming anew in a postmodern world', in S. Miller, M. Hubble and B. Duncan (eds), *Handbook of Solution-Focused Brief Therapy*. San Francisco: Jossey-Bass.

Warner, R.E. (1996) 'Counsellor bias against short term counselling: a comparison of counsellor and client satisfaction in a Canadian setting', *International Journal for the Advancement of Counselling*, 18: 153–62.

Washburn, P. (1994) 'Advantages of a brief solution-oriented focus in home-based family preservation services', *Journal of Systemic Therapies*, 13 (2): 47–58.

Watzlawick, P. (1984) *The Invented Reality*. New York: W.W. Norton.

Watzlawick, P., Weakland, J. and Fisch, R. (1974) *Change: Principles of Problem Formation and Problem Resolution*. New York: W.W. Norton.

Weakland, J., Fisch, R., Watzlawick, P. and Bodin, A. (1974) 'Brief therapy: focused problem resolution', *Family Process*, 13: 141–68.

Weakland, J. and Jordan, L. (1992) 'Working briefly with reluctant clients: child protective services as an example', *Journal of Family Therapy*, 14: 231–54.

Webster, D. (1990) 'Solution-focused approaches in psychiatric/mental health nursing', *Perspectives in Psychiatric Care*, 26 (4): 17–21.

Weiner-Davis, M., de Shazer, S. and Gingerich, W. (1987) 'Building on pretreatment change to construct the therapeutic solution: an exploratory study', *Journal of Marital and Family Therapy*, 13 (4): 359–63.

Wells, R. and Gianetti, V. (eds) (1993) *Casebook of the Brief Psychotherapies*. New York: Plenum Press.

Wetchler, J.L. (1990) 'Solution-focused supervision', *Family Therapy*, 17 (2): 129–38.

Wheeler, J. (2003) 'Solution-focused practice in social work', in B. O'Connell and S. Palmer, *Handbook of Solution-Focused Therapy*. London: Sage.

White, M. (1988) 'The process of questioning: a therapy of literary merit?', *Dulwich Newsletter*, Summer: 3–21.

White, M. (1989) *Selected Papers*. Adelaide: Dulwich Centre Publications.

White, M. (1993) 'Deconstruction and therapy', in S. Gilligan and R. Price (eds), *Therapeutic Conversations*. New York: W.W. Norton.

White, M. (1995) *Re-authoring Lives: Interviews and Essays*. Adelaide: Dulwich Centre Publications.

White, M. and Epston, D. (1990) *Narrative Means to Therapeutic Ends*. New York: W.W. Norton.

White, N. (2003) 'The solution-focused approach in higher education', in B. O'Connell and S. Palmer, *Handbook of Solution-Focused Therapy*. London: Sage.

Widdicombe, S. (1993) 'Autobiography and change: rhetoric and authenticity of "Gothic" style', in E. Burman and I. Parker (eds), *Discourse Analysis Research*. London: Routledge.

Wilgosh, R. (1993) 'How can we see where we're going if we're always looking backwards?' *Counselling*, 4 (2): 98–101.

Wilkins, P. (1993) 'Person-centred therapy and the person-centred approach: a personal view', *Counselling*, 4 (1): 31–2.

Zimmerman, T.S., Prest, L.A. and Wetzel, B.E. (1997) 'Solution-focused couples therapy groups: an empirical study', *Journal of Family Therapy*, 19: 125–44.

Index

'absent clients' 107
abuse survivors 139
acceptance 82
accreditation of therapists 38
achievements 61
action stage 119–20
advantages of SFT 131–2
aims
  first session 37
  second session 64–5
  see also principles
ambivalence 66, 103, 120
anxiety 125
applications of SFT 131–9
assessment for therapy 26, 104
assumptions
  minimising 19
  SFT 24, 29–32
  therapeutic stances 9
attentiveness 81
attitudes to change 27–8, 43
automatic thoughts 122
autonomy 111

behaviour
  feelings relationship 46, 102–3
  problem manifestation 35, 45, 49
belief systems 74, 121
beneficence 111
between-session work 80
  see also tasks
BFTC *see* Brief Family
  Therapy Center
'big I' exercise 23
blame 77
brain sides 123
Brief Family Therapy Center (BFTC)
  1, 5, 7, 18, 112
brief therapy 1–6, 79, 103–4, 115
British Association for Counselling
  and Psychotherapy 89

case study example 82–5
causality 13–14
CBT *see* cognitive-behavioural therapy

change
  amplification 30
  attitudes to 27–8, 43
  causes 41
  climate for 39–45
  consolidation 65–7
  expectancy of 3
  future orientation 7
  incremental 31, 47
  internal attribution 66
  major 73
  negative effects 32, 66
  ongoing 19, 81
  pre-session 33–4, 39–41
  strategies 72–3
  sustaining 32, 67
change discourse 33–5, 86
characteristics
  brief therapy 2–3, 115
  constructionism 11–13
  Employee Assistance Programmes 135
  Erickson's therapy 16
  long-term therapy 3
  solution-focused organisations 133, 136
child protection 138–9
chronic conditions 104, 137
chronic fatigue syndrome (ME) 43
circular questions 51
client group examples 18
clients
  dependency 59, 78
  expectations 5–6, 15–16, 22, 24, 26, 38
  involuntary 105–7
  preferences 1, 5–6
  priorities 6
  resources 36, 40, 56–60, 104–5
  types 26–8, 120
  uniqueness 64, 104
climate for change 39–45
cognitive-behavioural therapy
  (CBT) 120–2
collaboration 3, 7–8
  first session 37–9
  focal issue 28
  narrative negotiation 14

collaboration *cont.*
  opening gambits 20
  solution discourse 35
  supervision 90
  see also 'joining'
common language 28
competence focus
  supervision 90, 92–3, 96
  therapy 8, 29–31, 34, 56–7
'complainant' client type 26–7, 120
complex conditions 104
compliance 68
confidence 22, 36
consolidating change 65–7
construct testing 77–8
constructionism 9–15, 75–6, 91, 104
  see also language; meaning
constructive failure 65, 93
  see also failed solutions
contemplation stage 119–20
context-based perspectives 9
context-changing talk 34
context sensitivity 74, 80
contracting 24–6
coping questions 87
coping strategies 68, 129
couple counselling 52
cross-cultural work 111–12
crying 75–6
cultural conditioning 43
curiosity 82, 90
'customer' client type 26–7, 120
customised strategies 24
cycle of change model 119–20

deconstructing problems 73–8
defence mechanisms 23
deliberate exceptions 57–8
dependency 19, 59, 78
depression 76–7
descriptive language 44–5
descriptive versus explanatory data 19
destructive beliefs 121
dialogic ecology 30
diary keeping 122, 124
discipline 81
discourse analysis 30
discourse types 33
'do something different' task
    63, 125, 128, 134
drama 123–4
drawing 124

EAPs *see* Employee Assistance
    Programmes
Eastern philosophy 43
ecological stage of theory development 8
education 135–7
effectiveness 3–5
efficient causality 13
empathy 35, 38–9, 82, 86
  see also validating client perspectives
Employee Assistance Programmes
    (EAPs) 134–5
empowerment
  exceptions 59
  future orientation 7
  length of treatment 25
  pre-session change 40
  scaling questions 70
  unburdening 65
'empty chair' exercise 124
endings 78–9, 95, 97
epistemology 8–9
Erickson, Milton 16
essentialist stage of theory development 8
Ethical Framework (2003) 89
ethical issues 89, 91, 93, 111
evaluation 67, 78–9
exception seeking 57–60, 92
exception talk 34
exercises 23, 43–4, 124, 126, 127
  see also tasks
expectations
  change 3
  clients 5–6, 15–16, 22, 24, 26, 38
  therapists 6
experiential techniques 122–6
experimentation 65, 67
explanations 121–2
  see also language
explanatory versus descriptive data 19
exploring tasks 60–3
external parties 41, 55, 107
externalisation 76–7, 117, 125–6

face value acceptance 110
failed solutions 15–16, 32, 36,
    45, 59, 72–3
  see also constructive failure
family counselling 52
fantasy 126
FAQs (frequently asked questions) 102–13
feedback 60–3, 66
feelings–behaviour relationship 46, 102–3

female clients/therapists 112–13
FFST *see* formula first session task
fidelity 111
final causality 13
first session 37–63, 83
five-stage cycle of change model 119–20
five-stage supervision model 95–7
focal issues 28–9, 65
force-field analysis 127–8
formula first session task (FFST) 62, 68
foundations of SFT 7–17
frequency of sessions 1, 4, 25–6
frequently asked questions (FAQs) 102–13
future orientation 7, 13–15, 21, 22, 97

genuineness 82
goals
    clarification 46–56
    feedback 62
    identification 3, 16, 20, 36
    session 96
    supervision 95
    treatment versus life 78
ground rules 129
groupwork 52, 126, 131–2

health work 137–8
holistic approach 137
humour 82
hypothesis testing 77

iceberg metaphor 21
ideology
    absence of 114
    commitment to 25
illustrating scales 70
imagination 47, 128–9
'in a word' exercise 127
inclusivity of profession 90
incremental change 31, 36, 47
influencing 118
integrated approach 114–30
intellectual understanding 66–7, 123
internal attribution 66
interpersonal skills 42, 81–2
intervention types 85–8
involuntary clients 105–7

'joining' 24–5, 76, 118, 130
    see also collaboration
journal keeping 122, 124
justice 111

knowledge perspectives 9

labelling 74
'land of the giants' exercise 126
language
    meaning construction 16–17, 21,
        24, 30, 74, 118
    of therapy 28, 41, 44–5
    see also constructionism; explanations
learned helplessness 68
learning strategies 67
left-sided brain activity 123
length of treatment 2, 18, 23, 25
letter writing 124–6
long-term therapy 1, 3, 31, 79

maintenance stage 119–20
    see also sustaining change
major changes 73
Malan, D.H. 1
mandated clients 105–7
ME (chronic fatigue syndrome) 43
meaning
    construction 9–17, 21, 24, 30, 74, 118
    crying 75–6
    desire for 74
    see also constructionism; problems; 'truth'
medical model 9
Mental Research Institute (MRI)
        model 15–17, 45, 111
'the message' 60–3
minimal intervention principle
        18–19, 32, 81
miracle question 35, 47–52, 69, 83, 86–7
    case study example 83
    dramatisation 123
    drawing 124
    organisations 133–4
    revisiting 69
    supervision 93–4
misuses of SFT 42
model overview 18–36
modern perspectives 9
motivation 55–6
motivational interviewing 103
MRI *see* Mental Research Institute
multicultural communities 43, 111
multiple choice questions 87
multiple problems 28–9

naming the problem 42–3
narrative negotiation 14–15, 35

narrowing focus 65
negative change 32
negative forces 127–8
non-attributes, constructionism 12
non-expert (one down) position
      25, 43, 50, 80, 91, 111–12
non-maleficence 111
non-problematic focus 8, 22, 29, 59
note-taking 81–2
notice tasks 62
number of sessions 2, 18, 23, 25

objective reality 9
one down (non-expert) position
      25, 43, 50, 80, 91, 111–12
One-to-One Supervision 95–7
ongoing change 19, 81
opening gambits 20
organisations 133–4
overview of model 18–36

panic attacks 57, 125
passive victimhood 68
past-oriented interventions 22
peer support 97–101
person-centred therapy 115–18
personal construct counselling 77
'phantom traffic jam'
      phenomenon 22–3
placebo effect 115
positive feedback 60–1
positive forces 127–8
postmodernism see constructionism
practice points 17, 36, 88, 113
      brief therapy 6
      first session 63
      second/subsequent sessions 79
      supervision 101
practitioners 80–8
      see also therapists; user groups
pre-contemplation stage 119–20
pre-session change 33–4, 39–41, 96
predictions 69
preferences 1, 5–6
preparation stage 119–20
presenters 98–9
pretend tasks 63
previous therapeutic experience 37
principles 29–32
      see also aims
priorities 6

problem-focused approaches
      13–14, 19–23, 44
problem-solving techniques 127–8
problem-talk 129
problems
      deconstruction 73–8
      definition 2–3, 11, 21, 35
      reframing 75–6, 125–6
process managers 98
process model 32–6, 82–5
progress evaluation 110
psychological maps 14

qualities see interpersonal skills
questions
      'absent clients' 108
      change discourse 34
      circular 51
      climate of change 41–2
      coping 87
      ending/after-care 78
      exceptions 59
      FAQs 102–13
      force-field analysis 128
      goal clarification 46
      multiple choice 87
      problem-versus solution-focused 19–23
      progress 110
      scaling 53–6, 70–2
      second/subsequent sessions 67
      setbacks 73
      supervision 92–7
      see also miracle question

randomised tasks 62–3
rapport 35, 85–6
reality perspectives 9
recognition of success 22
reflection 91, 100
reframing problems 35, 75–6, 125–6
repetition of failed solutions 15
research reviews 4–5
resistance 23
resources 6, 40, 56–60, 104–5
right-sided brain activity 123
risk taking 65
rock climbing metaphor 64

scaling 35
      CBT 121
      dramatisation 123

scaling *cont.*
    drawing 124
    endings 78–9
    first session 52–6
    health work 138
    second/subsequent sessions 69–72
    supervision 94–5, 97
second/subsequent sessions 64–79, 83–5
self-fulfilling prophecies 122
sensitive situations 51–2
sentence completion 86
setbacks 72–3, 84
simplicity 32
single-session therapy 4
six-stage supervision model 99–101
social constructionism *see*
    constructionism
social work 138–9
socio-economic status 18
solution construction 69–72
solution discourse 33, 35, 86–7
solution-'forced' therapy 42
spontaneous exceptions 58
spontaneous improvement 57
strategic counselling 103, 111
strategy discourse 33, 36, 87–8
structure of therapy 4, 25
success recognition 22
suitability assessment 26, 104
supervision 89–101
sustaining change 32, 67
    see also maintenance stage
'symptoms' 18, 107–9, 125–6

tasks
    assignment 36, 62–3
    'do something different' 63, 125,
        128, 134
    formula first session task 62, 68
    performance 68
    see also between-session work; exercises
team supervision 97–101
teams 134
'technical eclecticism' 114
terminal illness 137–8
testing constructs 77–8

TFA (thinking, feeling, acting)
    model 118–19
theoretical orientation 115
theory development 8, 114
therapeutic letter writing 124–6
therapists
    accreditation 38
    expectations 6
    ideological commitment 25
    interpersonal skills 81–2
    learning from client 8, 25
    one down (non-expert)
        position 25, 43, 50
    priorities 6
    supervision 89–101
    see also practitioners
thinking, feeling, acting (TFA) model 118–19
time-sensitive therapy 2
timing 42, 66, 81
transitional stage of theory development 8
'truth' 10, 11, 16–17, 30, 74
    see also meaning
two islands exercise 43–4, 124

unburdening 65
underestimating abilities 73
'underlying issues' 107–9
uniqueness of clients 64, 104
unused solutions 69
unwilling clients 105–7
user groups 2, 8, 80, 131, 133, 137

validating client perspectives 16, 22,
        30, 103, 107, 111
    see also empathy
values, person-centred approach 116–17
vicious circles 15, 21
'visitor' client type 26–7, 120

waiting lists 2
warmth 82
Western philosophy 43
'what else' prompt 49
women 112–13
workplace teams 134
writing 124–6

Compiled by INDEXING SPECIALISTS (UK) Ltd., Regent House, Hove Street, Hove, East Sussex BN3 2DW. Tel: 01273 738299. E-mail: richardr@indexing.co.uk Website: www.indexing.co.uk